Vocal Direction for the Theatre

From Script Analysis to Opening Night

Vocal Direction for the Theatre

From Script Analysis to Opening Night

By

Nan Withers-Wilson

Drama Book Publishers
New York

Library of Congress Cataloging-in-Publication Data
Withers-Wilson, Nan.
    Vocal direction for the theatre : from script analysis to opening
night / by Nan Withers-Wilson.
        p.   cm.
    Includes index.
    ISBN 0-89676-122-3 : $19.95
    1. Voice culture.   2. Speech.   3. Acting.   4. Theater—Production
and direction.   I. Title.
PN2071.S65W58   1993
808.5—dc20   93-14880
                                                         CIP

This book is dedicated with love to Jonathan Wilson, Marge Biersach, my family, and the many theatre artists and students who, over the years, have been my teachers and constant source of inspiration.

Contents

Acknowledgments

I would like to express my heartfelt gratitude to the following individuals whose knowledge, expertise, and generous assistance have contributed to the writing of *Vocal Direction for the Theatre:*

Dr. Robert Bastian, otolaryngologist and professor in the Department of Otolaryngology—Head and Neck Surgery at the Loyola University of Chicago Medical Center, Maywood, Illinois; Fran Bennett, Professor of Voice Production, California Institute of the Arts, Valencia, California; Dr. James Coakley, Professor of Theatre, Northwestern University, Evanston, Illinois; Carol Pendergrast, Professor of Theatre, East Carolina University, Greenville, North Carolina; Jonathan Wilson, Professor of Theatre, Loyola University Chicago, and director, SSDC; and Chris Phillips, scenic and lighting designer, USAA.

In addition, the author would like to thank the following for their permission to print the extracts included in this book:

Michael Imison Playwrights Ltd., 28 Almeida Street, London N1 1TD, Copyright Agent for the Estate of Noel Coward, for the extract from *Hay Fever* by Noel Coward, copyright © 1925, reprinted from the Samuel French, Inc. 1954 edition.

Penguin USA for the extract from *Tyrone Guthrie On Acting* by Tyrone Guthrie, copyright © 1971 by Tyrone Guthrie. Used by permission of Viking Penguin, a division of Penguin Books USA Inc.

Penguin USA for the extract from *Death of a Salesman* by Arthur Miller, copyright © 1949, renewed 1977 by Arthur Miller. Used by permission of Viking Penguin, a division of Penguin Books USA Inc.

International Creative Management, Inc. for the extract from *Death of a Salesman* by Arthur Miller, copyright © 1949 by Arthur Miller, renewed 1980 by Arthur Miller.

The Lucy Kroll Agency for extracts from *The Great White Hope* by Howard Sackler. *The Great White Hope* was originally produced by Herman Levin and directed by Edward Sherin at the Alvin Theatre in New York.

Introduction

Over the past thirty years a number of excellent texts have been published on the subject of voice and speech training for the actor. In recent years, two books by British authors—John Barton's *Playing Shakespeare* (1984) and Cicely Berry's *The Actor and His Text* (1987)—have provided welcome and insightful instruction for the actor on how to handle language in the theatre, especially the language of Shakespeare's plays. But conspicuously absent from the existing body of literature on voice for the theatre has been any account of how the theatre voice specialist functions as a collaborative artist within the production process.

Concerned by this fact, I began to record my own experiences and work methods as a vocal director for the theatre so that I might share with vocal directors, teachers of performance, actors, and directors the challenges and discoveries that I have encountered over the past eighteen years in working with actors' voices in production.

Except for theatre schools which are identified as having "pre-professional training programs," most theatre departments in America's colleges and universities tend to hire only one faculty member in the area of voice training for the actor. As a result, theatre voice teachers and vocal directors have had to work in relative isolation from their professional counterparts. In 1986 VASTA, the Voice and Speech Trainers Association, was founded. This organization concretely identified a group of individuals working in the field of voice for the theatre. The sense of isolation gone, my wish to communicate with my colleagues began to grow.

Vocal Direction for the Theatre has also been written for actors. Since the early 1970s, more and more opportunities have arisen for professional actors and students of acting to obtain voice training either through private study, through voice classes offered in professional training schools, or as part of college and university theatre programs.

It is not my intention to provide a book on vocal technique for the actor. Instead this book has been written to help the actor more fully understand the function of the vocal director in the theatre, to help define the collaborative nature of the actor/director/vocal director relationship in the production process, to explore the responsibilities of the actor in regard to the care and development of his own voice in both rehearsal and performance, and to illuminate anew the exciting challenges involved in the actor's creation of a character's vocal life for the stage.

Vocal Direction for the Theatre has been written as a resource for stage directors as well. Directing texts rarely deal with the problems and responsibilities that confront the stage director in regard to the actor's vocal life in rehearsal and performance. In the American theatre it is still the exception rather than the norm for a stage director to employ the assistance of a theatre voice specialist as a member of the production team. Many directors recognize the actors' need for voice and speech work, but are hesitant to engage the expertise of a vocal director due to a lack of understanding of that artist's function within the production process. A common perception among directors is that the vocal director works solely with the actors and is required only when dealing with a classical play or one that involves the use of dialects. *Vocal Direction for the Theatre* has been written to help directors understand the many ways in which a vocal director can assist actors, directors, and designers in developing the vocal life of *any* theatrical production and how stage directors can communicate more effectively with vocal directors as members of their production teams.

One of the reasons why the collaborative relationship between the stage director and the vocal director has been slow to achieve definition in the American theatre is due, in part, to the title that is commonly used to denote the theatre voice specialist working within the production process. What's in a name? In this instance, a great deal. In this text the title "vocal director" is utilized rather than the more frequently employed designation "vocal coach." The title "vocal coach" is a limited one, for the word "coach," meaning "to instruct or train," infers that the theatre voice specialist works solely with the actors during the rehearsal period. This inference has been a source of much confusion to stage directors and has had a negative impact upon the effective use of vocal directors within the production process.

The title "vocal director" is a more accurate and encompassing one. It corresponds in many respects to that of "musical director" as it has long been utilized in the musical theatre. Like the musical director, vocal directors for the theatre collaborate not only with the actors, but also with the director and the entire production team to insure that the language of the play is clearly and effectively communicated by the actors in production.

Finally, my decision to write *Vocal Direction for the Theatre* was influenced by my own experiences as an audience member. How often have I gone to the theatre and, while awaiting the start of the production, been inspired by the pre-show music and visual spectacle to say to myself, "Oh, this is going to be wonderful!" . . . only to have these initial feelings of awe and excitement dashed at the first sound of the actors' voices. This feeling of "let down" has occurred so frequently in my theatregoing experiences over the years that I realized it was not the fault of an isolated production or two, but a more pervasive problem within the American theatre; a problem related to the value and importance that actors and directors assign to a play's language and the actor's voice as the means of expressing that language.

An excellent visual production of a play is one in which an audience member can sit in the auditorium and discern the story of the play, the thoughts and feelings of the characters, and the characters' relationships to one another solely through what is being seen; like watching a film without the sound track. Similarly, one should be able to come to a theatrical production and, with eyes closed, grasp the story, the characters' thoughts and feelings, and the characters' relationships solely through the aural elements of the production.

In the final analysis the actor's voice is nothing but sound, but that sound carries to the audience a whole set of meanings. For the trained listener, an individual's speaking voice is an aural autobiography. The human voice can reveal such factors as sex, age, regional and geographic origins, state of mental and physical health, self-image, temperament, social class, ethnic origin, level of education, personal objectives, and the nature of an individual's interpersonal relationships. Even the untrained listener will make subjective judgments based upon the sound of a speaker's voice, instantly assessing the speaker's identity, worth, competence, intelligence level, objectives, and attitudes.

Given the fact that the actor's voice is so important in communicating to the audience the character's identity, thoughts, feelings, and relationships and that the actors' voices represent a major contribution to the aural impact of a theatrical production, why is the actor's vocal life often given so little attention in the rehearsal process? Why are we so often disappointed with the actors' voices in the plays we attend? Why are microphones being used more and more to amplify the voices of actors in nonmusical productions? Why has voice training not been an ever-present and integral part of the American actor's education?

The answers to these questions can be found, in part, by examining the history of voice and speech training for the American actor. The growing emergence of vocal directors as collaborative artists in the production process is an exciting part of this history and represents a significant movement toward establishing higher standards of vocal excellence in the theatre. But, as theatre is a collaborative art form, no one aspect of production can be viewed in isolation from the whole. The attainment of greater vocal excellence in the theatre will be achieved only through a renewed awareness, commitment, and collaborative effort on the part of all theatre artists, and it is for them that *Vocal Direction for the Theatre* has been written.

Chapter 1

The History of Voice and Speech Training for the American Actor

The Background

A study of the history of voice and speech training for the American actor during the 19th and 20th centuries reveals that, although the actor's use of his voice is inextricably connected to the art of acting, voice training has not always been viewed as integral to the education and development of American actors. It has been embraced or rejected in accordance with the mode of acting style and training presently in vogue. The value placed upon voice and speech training for the actor and the methods of approaching that training have long been topics of discussion and debate. Samplings of different opinions held by some of the important figures who have influenced the history of voice and speech training in America are:

> Why not leave nature to do her own work? Impress but the mind fully with the sentiments to be uttered; withdraw the attention from the sound, and fix it on the sense; and nature or habit, will spontaneously suggest the proper delivery.
>
> BISHOP RICHARD WHATELY
> *Elements of Rhetoric* (1828)[1]

> As a science, [elocution] unfolds the principles of reading and speaking; as an art, it embodies in delivery every accomplishment, both of voice and action, necessary to appropriate expression.
>
> S.S. HAMILL, A.M.
> *The Science of Elocution* (1872)[2]

> The trouble with bad delivery nine-tenths of the time is a failure to use the faculties of the mind, or a misuse of them in the act of speaking; and one reason why delivery has not been made better is this very fact that it has been considered merely a physical thing, separate from personality.
>
> SAMUEL SILAS CURRY
> *Province of Expression* (1891)[3]

Special teachers highly trained in the science of speech sounds and its practical application to the art of good pronunciation . . . constitute the advance guard in America's war on her poor, indistinct and inelegant speech, one of the greatest drawbacks in the development of her national refinement and culture.

MARGARET PRENDERGAST MCLEAN
Good American Speech (1928)[4]

We need firm foundations for our art . . . in particular the art of speech and the ability to speak verse. Musical speech opens up endless possibilities of conveying the inner life [we experience] on the stage . . . What can we express with . . . our ordinary register of five or six notes? . . . . We realize how ridiculous we are . . . [when] we have to convey complicated emotions. It is like playing Beethoven on a balalaika . . . . Speech is music. Pronunciation on the stage is as difficult an art as singing. It requires training and a technique bordering on virtuosity. . . . When an actor adds the vivid ornament of sound to the living content of the words, he causes me to glimpse with an inner vision the images he has fashioned out of his own creative imagination. . . . To an actor a word is not just a sound, it is the evocation of images. . . . Your job [as an actor] is to instill your inner vision in others and convey it in words.

KONSTANTIN STANISLAVSKY
Building A Character (1949)[5]

The idea of the American Academy of Dramatic Arts has always been to work from within: to build the idea, the concept, the truth of the character and scene—and let the form of expression follow naturally . . . . The Academy ideal and the Stanislavsky ideal are much the same, but Stanislavsky formalized the method of responding while the Academy has not.

ARISTIDE D'ANGELO
Interview with Garff Wilson, (1939)[6]

The simplest thing that an actor does is to speak. The author has already made a kind of logic in the lines. Often the actor need only do the simple carrying out of tasks and the simple conveying of the meaning of the words. . . . Today we are in a period that is nonvocal and non-expressive. Today we feel a lot of things we do not have words to say. Our English is literally poor in quantity as well as quality. We don't have a wide enough vocabulary. Today you will find much greater vitality in ordinary speech than in intellectual speech. Bums have a very rich vocabulary. The concept of good speech today implies impersonality and politeness. . . .

LEE STRASBERG
Strasberg at the Actors Studio (1965)[7]

The search by actors for the truth within themselves has now gone too far. . . . The Methodists overprize the search for truth as opposed to the revelation of truth. They have neglected the means of communication.

TYRONE GUTHRIE
In Various Directions (1965)[8]

No standards of "correct" speech will be given [in my text]. Such standards last longer between the covers of a book than on the tongues of living people and are a lost cause because live communication will not sit still and behave. Much of what, in the past, was hopefully labeled Standard American, Transatlantic Speech or Standard English, was a reflection of class consciousness and as an attempted aesthetic rule of thumb is doomed to failure. Yesterday's beauty becomes today's camp and today's ugliness may pass for tomorrow's ultimate truth.

KRISTIN LINKLATER
Freeing the Natural Voice (1976)[9]

Throughout the history of the American theatre, methods of voice and speech training for the actor have undergone continual change. When these methods have been in harmony with the prevailing modes of actor expression, they have been adopted as an integral part of the actor's education. But, when approaches to voice and speech training have been at odds with the acting style and repertory of plays popular in a given period, acting teachers have discouraged their pupils from engaging in voice and speech training, and actors have neglected the development and care of this critical aspect of their artistic expression.

The Origin of the Elocution Movement

In the nineteenth and early twentieth centuries, actors were schooled in the art of vocal delivery known as elocution. Regarded as both an art and a science, elocution was developed in England in the mid-eighteenth century as a means of enhancing the reading and speaking skills of clergy, lawyers, political leaders, and public speakers.

Thomas Sheridan and John Walker, two leaders of the elocutionary movement, looked to the theatre for models of effective delivery on which to base their teaching. The British theatre at mid-century was enjoying a renewed popularity due, in part, to the presence and influence of the great actor David Garrick (1717–79). Garrick rejected the prevailing neoclassic approach to acting with its use of formal gesture and oratory and introduced a more realistic acting style characterized by a greater simplicity of manner and diction. Sheridan and Walker analyzed Garrick's performance style and utilized their findings as a basis for teaching elocution. Thomas Sheridan defined the art of elocution as follows:

> A just delivery consists in a distinct articulation of words, pronounced in proper tones, suitably varied to the sense, and the emotions of the mind; with due observation of accent; of emphasis, in its several gradations; of rests or pauses of the voice, in proper place and well-measured degrees of time; and the whole accompanied with expressive looks, and significant gesture. [10]

The fact that Garrick's vocal expression was so highly regarded by the elocutionists of the period raises an important point in regard to the evolution of voice and speech instruction for the actor from 1750 to the present. With few exceptions, the creators of methodologies for training the actor's voice have been motivated by an attempt to create a manner of delivery that is true to nature. Though the elaborate rules and systems of notation that the elocutionists put down as guidelines for vocal and physical expression now seem to us stilted and mechanical, they were formulated in an attempt to provide a systematic means by which the actor/speaker could more realistically and effectively convey the emotions and attitudes embodied in the written word:

> It was the elocutionists' primary claim to fame in rhetorical history that they applied the tenets of science to the physiological phenomena of spoken discourse, making great contributions to human knowledge in the process. . . . The methodology of the elocutionary movement, like that of science, was a combination of observing and recording. Just as the astronomer observed the movements of the planets and recorded them in special symbols, so the elocutionists observed certain phenomena of voice, body, and language, and recorded them in systems of notation. . . . The philosophy of the elocutionary movement, like that of the scientific-rationalistic creed, was a conception of man controlled by natural law. The elocutionists believed that the nature of man was governed by the same law and order which seventeenth century science had discovered in the nature of the universe. They could claim that their rules and principles and systems represented the order that is found in nature; they were "nature still, but nature methodized." [11]

The Elocutionary Movement in America

From 1750, the books of British elocutionists were published and utilized in America. The first significant American contribution to the field was
made by Dr. James Rush whose book The *Philosophy of the Human Voice* was
published in 1827. Dr. Rush's text not only dealt with the rules and principles of effective delivery, but also provided a scientific description of the
physiology of vocal production and a system of notating speech sounds. Dr.
Rush's work merged the science of medicine with the art of elocution. The
Philosophy of the Human Voice promoted interest in elocutionary training in
America's educational institutions and increased the demand for private
teachers of elocution. Respect for Rush's work declined in academic institutions at mid-century, however, as elocution became increasingly viewed as
an art for public performers. Many teachers of elocution, lacking a scientific
understanding of the physiology of vocal production, taught a simplified
version of Rush's system, which ignored the cultivation of vocal health,
flexibility, and stamina. Instead, their teachings set rules for conveying
thought and emotion through a mechanical and external manipulation of the
voice along with prescribed physical postures and facial expressions. This
distortion of Rush's teachings, coupled with the fact that Rush's treatise on
Elements of the Philosophy of the Human Mind—a document that puts forth the
important linkage between the influence of the mind upon human speech—
was not published until 1865, led to the derision of Rush's system. According
to Lester Hale in his article "Dr. James Rush":

> The fact that Rush wrote at all in the field of speech was rather accidental.
> Yet once [Rush had] demonstrated that human vocal expression could be
> observed in minute detail and given an orderly and systematic description,
> he established a precedent which lesser men than he were to abuse. Rush
> did not plan a prescriptive system for teachers of elocution, but intended
> to show nature's orderly design. That he should have given impetus to a
> trend towards mechanical artifice of communication and aesthetic art was
> an unhappy ending to a noble determination to discover scientific facts
> about human behavior. [12]

Unlike the "lesser men" who simplified and distorted the teachings of
Dr. Rush, the renowned American actor, writer, and teacher James Murdoch
(1811–93) sought to accurately convey the true value of Rush's discoveries.
Wishing to improve the quality of his own speaking voice, Murdoch came
under Rush's tutelage and was so impressed with the doctor's methods of

vocal training that he himself became a teacher of Rush's theories. Throughout his fifty-year career as a leader in the elocutionary movement, Murdoch
proclaimed the validity of the voice training principles put forth in *The
Philosophy of the Human Voice* and his conviction that, using Rush's methods,
the speaking voice, like the singing voice, could be trained in strength,
quality, flexibility, and expression. A number of Murdoch's students went
on to become prominent and influential teachers of elocution and oratory in
American universities in the late 1800s.

Elocution prevailed as a method of teaching vocal delivery to the actor
throughout the nineteenth century for a number of reasons. The pervasive
"star system" did little to encourage spontaneous interaction between actors
on the stage.[13] In the absence of a director to guide the actor in the creation
of a character for the stage, elocution provided the actor with a concrete set
of rules with which to analyze the text and orchestrate the vocal and physical
interpretation of a role for performance.[14] Also, the highly theatrical use of
the voice that elocution encouraged—the pear-shaped vowels and the orotund
tones—lent itself to the classic school of acting that existed on the American
stage throughout the nineteenth century. Great actors and actresses of the
classic school such as Charlotte Cushman, Mary Ann Duff, James Murdoch,
and Edwin Booth "trained their voices to be flexible, responsive, and varied,
so that their elocution was characterized by correct pronunciation and skillful
management of cadence and poetic rhythm. . . . They valued the art of
elocution and worked constantly to perfect the beauty and clarity of their
speech."[15]

In the late nineteenth century, plays by European naturalistic and realistic playwrights were introduced into the American theatre and had a
profound influence on the actors who performed them. The presentational
and declamatory nature of the elocutionary approach to acting that had served
the heroic tragedies, romantic dramas, and sensational melodramas was found
to be no longer appropriate. The naturalistic and realistic playwrights created
characters determined by the forces of heredity and environment, whose
identities were more effectively revealed on the stage through well-motivated
and true-to-life speech and action.

In her book *Voice in the Modern Theatre*, Jacqueline Martin points out
that "with the advent of naturalism in the theatre, a general deterioration in
elocution was the result, and the attitude to speaking blank verse by strictly
following the metre gave way to regarding it as prose. A declining interest
in the Elocutionary Movement and an increasing number of scientific exper-
iments in speech and acting towards the end of the 1800s were responsible
for elocution coming to be regarded as a science rather than an art."[16]

In the late nineteenth century, the increasing interest in the science of psychology inspired a new form of elocution in America known as "expression" in which the workings of the mind played an influential role in determining vocal utterance. The expression movement was founded by Samuel Silas Curry, Ph.D., a student of Steele Mackaye,[17] a minister and a professor of oratory at Boston University. Although Curry admired Rush's scientific findings regarding the voice, he rejected the mechanical and didactic approach that had become associated with Rush's system, and insisted on changing the name of his methodology of voice training from elocution to expression. Curry's main contribution to the study of elocution was that of psychology. He perceived the interconnection between the mind, voice, and body and "was the first teacher to advocate specific training for the mind. He [felt] that the cause (the mind) must be trained as well as the means (body and voice) to achieve the effect desired (effective delivery)."[18]

After retiring from Boston University in 1888, Dr. Curry served as head of the School of Expression in Boston until his death in 1921. With the increasing influence of realism in the theatre, expression became the favored mode of voice and speech training for the actor at the turn of the century.

The various forms of elocutionary training that evolved out of the nineteenth century shared in common the beliefs that art must be based on science and that the purpose of training was the effective outer expression of inner thought and emotion. Teachers and students in the private schools of elocution and expression in the late nineteenth century were to influence America's voice and speech education in the twentieth century for many years. Giles Wilkeson Gray writes that:

> The three decades from 1890 and 1920 were a period of transition in the development of American speech education. . . . It was during these years that all the various aspects of oral communication were drawn together and integrated, under the common rubric of *speech*.
>
> Work on the drama, heretofore primarily an extracurricular activity, was brought back into the classroom and given a prominent place in the speech curriculum. Delivery was elevated from the mechanized systems growing out of the philosophies of Diderot, Engel, Walker, Austin, Rush, and Delsarte, and made an integral aspect of the study of speech. . . . The teaching of speech had moved from the itinerant elocutionist and the private schools, interested in public performance as a form of entertainment, to the high schools, the colleges, and the universities, and had become a respected academic discipline with status equal to that of any other subject in the curriculum.[19]

Voice and Speech Training for the Actor in the Twentieth Century

In the early twentieth century the study of voice and speech in America was altered by another significant influence—the science of phonetics. Phonetics is that branch of language study dealing with speech sounds, their production and combination, and their representation by written symbols. Speaking of the practical value of phonetics, Henry Sweet (1845–1912), the renowned British linguist and phonetician, stated that phonetics could not only serve as a valuable tool in learning the correct pronunciation of foreign languages, but could assist the native speaker in eradicating "vulgarisms and provincialisms of pronunciation and secure uniformity of speech."[20]

A major spokesman for the science of phonetics in America was the English phonetician William Tilly. Professor Tilly had studied with Henry Sweet in England and, in 1918, came to America to teach at Columbia University in New York City. The teaching and writings of Professor Tilly's students influenced the teaching of speech throughout America. Two of these students—Margaret Prendergast McClean (1878–1961) and Edith Warman Skinner (d. 1981)—were to have a profound effect upon the voice and speech training of American actors.

Margaret Prendergast McClean became nationally known in the 1920s as a leading authority in dramatic interpretation and Theatre Speech (also known as Mid-Atlantic or Transatlantic). Just as the science of psychology had influenced S.S. Curry's School of Expression, Mrs. McClean expressed that the science of phonetics "is the only way pronunciation can be properly studied and accurately represented."[21] Her book *Good American Speech*, first published in 1928, became a popular text used in American high schools, universities, and drama schools. In it she stresses that a sound knowledge of the science of phonetics can assist students in acquiring good American speech free from regionalisms. She observed that, "[While] phonetics will not provide the heart and soul and spirit that gives all speech its real significance, it will, however, enable the speaker to express his thoughts clearly, forcefully and convincingly, and help him to 'utter his heart' with simplicity and beauty."[22]

According to Edith Skinner, Mrs. McClean's influence upon voice and speech training in the American theatre commenced in the 1920s when she began working with the Moscow Art Theatre actor/teacher Richard Boleslavsky at the American Laboratory Theatre in New York City.

> [Richard Boleslavsky] asked Professor Tilly to send him someone who could teach his students how to sound Irish in a play that he was doing

[called] *Juno and the Paycock.* Tilly sent Margaret McLean, who I later
assisted, to train the students to speak an Irish dialect. When it was
completed, Boleslavsky . . . said to his students, "Well, if you can speak
in the Irish dialect, why don't you learn to speak your own language."
From that point on, in Richard Boleslavsky's school, good speech began
to be taught in the American Theatre.[23]

Throughout the 1920s, 30s, and 40s Theatre Speech or Transatlantic
was taught in America's professional acting schools. It represented a neutral
dialect that borrowed from both Standard British and Standard American
pronunciations. Standard British is that variety of English associated with
the educated and/or upper classes of England and which is taught, and therefore perpetuated, in England's elite public schools (the equivalent of America's private academic institutions). Standard American is that variety of
American speech that is devoid of regional or ethnic characteristics and does
not reveal the geographical or cultural origins of the speaker. Standard American speech is that employed by the majority of educated persons in America,
and its pronunciation is recorded in our semi-authoritarian dictionaries as
first or preferred.

It is evident that theatre speech teachers of the period did not regard
Standard American speech as being "grand" enough to suffice as an aesthet-
ically acceptable mode of theatrical linguistic expression. Transatlantic
speech, which includes among its phonetic characteristics the use of the
British r-drop and selective use of the intermediate [a] sound as opposed to
the Standard American [æ] sound in words such as "last," "path," and
"dance," became the preferred mode of speech taught within professional
drama schools. Though Transatlantic bore many similarities to that mode of
speech employed by the American eastern upper class, it was in actuality a
manufactured dialect utilized solely by individuals who made the effort to
acquire it. Transatlantic or Theatre Speech was employed by the great stage
actors of the period such as Ethel Barrymore, Katharine Cornell, Alfred Lunt,
Lynn Fontanne, and Helen Hayes. When talking films were introduced in
1927, actors wishing to work in the movies rushed to obtain instruction in
this elevated mode of pronunciation (as is humorously depicted in the film
Singin' in the Rain). Robert Hobbs' *Teach Yourself Transatlantic* and Edith
Skinner's *The Seven Points for Good Speech in Classic Plays* are two texts that
provide instruction for the Transatlantic dialect, and it can be readily heard
in numerous films from the 1930s and 1940s which include performances by
actors such as Bette Davis, Katharine Hepburn, and Tyrone Power.

In 1923 the Moscow Art Theatre, under the direction of Konstantin
Stanislavsky, toured America. American theatregoers were deeply impressed

with the company's realistic character portrayals and their ensemble approach to acting. In 1924 Stanislavsky's *My Life in Art* was published in America. Between 1924 and 1929, the Russian acting teacher Richard Boleslavsky, assisted by two former members of the Moscow Art Theatre—Maria Ouspenskaya and Maria Germanova—taught the principles of the Stanislavsky System at the American Laboratory Theatre in New York City. Included among the school's other course offerings were phonetics and voice production.

Attending classes at the American Laboratory Theatre in 1927 were three individuals—Lee Strasberg, Stella Adler, and Harold Clurman—who would go on to make significant contributions to the Stanislavsky System's absorption into the mainstream of American actor training. In 1931 Strasberg, Clurman, and Cheryl Crawford started The Group Theatre which had as its goal the production of new plays written by American playwrights about Americans. In *The Fervent Years,* Harold Clurman wrote:

> The Group Theatre believed in a permanent company in which man was to be the measure of all things. . . . A technique of the theatre had to be founded on life values. . . our interest in the life of our times must lead us to discovery of those methods that would most truly convey this life through the theatre.[24]

The challenge of finding a common approach for The Group's acting style was assumed by Lee Strasberg who used The Group's actors to develop his own method of actor training. Renouncing the prevailing "star system" of New York's commercial theatre, the company sought to institute an ensemble approach to acting akin to what they had observed in the Moscow Art Theatre's touring company. The Group Theatre's commitment to the production of indigenous American plays by Americans and about Americans meant that most of the characters portrayed did not speak in a Standard American or Transatlantic dialect. The characters in The Group Theatre's productions of Clifford Odets' *Awake and Sing, Waiting for Lefty,* and *Golden Boy,* for example, were not grand kings and queens nor tuxedoed and gowned members of high society. They were common men and women whose voices needed to reflect their regional and ethnic origins. The company's acquisition of a standardized mode of pronunciation was, therefore, not a value embraced by the leaders of The Group Theatre. It is interesting to note that Clurman and Strasberg themselves possessed strong regional/ethnic accents, and they produced and directed many plays about characters who, by and large, spoke as they did.

In the quest to achieve "true emotion," Strasberg evolved an approach to actor training that placed heavy emphasis upon emotion memory exercises and the actors' exploration of their own inner resources. In 1934, Stella Adler studied with Stanislavsky in Paris "for more than a month, in sessions which sometimes lasted from four to five hours a day."[25] In doing so, she became the only member of the Group to work with Stanislavsky directly. She reported back to The Group's membership that Stanislavsky advocated the use of given circumstances and the "magic if" as levers for character creation rather than the use of emotion memory. She told them how Stanislavsky had advised against overemphasizing the use of the actor's personal life in the creation of a role. Strasberg responded by saying that Stanislavsky was wrong and that the "Strasberg Method," not the "Stanislavsky System," was more suitable for American actors.[26]

The Group Theatre produced some 20 productions between 1931 and 1940. Of these plays, only three or four were considered strong commercial successes, notably Clifford Odet's *Awake and Sing* (1935), *Waiting for Lefty* (1935), and *Golden Boy* (1937) and Sidney Kingsley's *Men In White* (1933). Although The Group Theatre eventually ran out of plays to produce and money to produce them, its leaders held to the theatre's initial goal to produce only original American plays. According to Elia Kazan, this refusal on the part of The Group's leadership to consider productions of the classics was not only due to their commitment to produce only plays that would "reflect the life of their times," but also to a lack of technical skills in certain of their membership who possessed strong regional and ethnic accents:

> We weren't equipped to do the god damn classics. Look at my speech. How would we sound? Ridiculous. We were what we were. That was a good thing about The Group. We were out of New York and spoke that language and had those preoccupations and had felt those struggles.[27]

The heritage of The Group Theatre and its influence on actor training in America was to be passed on to future generations as many of its members went on to become America's leading acting teachers, directors, and designers in theatre and film.

In 1936, two years before his death, Stanislavksy's *An Actor Prepares* was published in America. This book, focusing upon the actor's internal technique and psychology, was viewed by those who advocated the Strasberg "Method" as evidence that Stanislavsky stressed the importance of internal over external technique. Stanislavsky's *Building A Character,* which deals with the external technical skills required of the actor in the performance of a role, was written in the 1930s, but, due to World War II, was not published in America until 1949. Only then did the full scope of Stanislavsky's teachings become evident. In *Building A Character* Stanislavsky makes clear the need for extensive voice training to enable the actor to vocally convey his character to the audience. But the long period of time that separated the publications of these two volumes had a profound effect upon American actor training. In the thirteen years between the appearance of *An Actor Prepares* and *Building A Character,* the Strasberg "Method," with its emphasis upon emotion memory and the actor's use of his own personal experience in the creation of a role, had taken a strong hold on the American approach to actor training.

In 1947 Robert Lewis, Cheryl Crawford, and Elia Kazan organized the Actors Studio in New York City as a training ground for professional actors, and, in 1951, Kazan asked Lee Strasberg to join the Studio faculty. Strasberg described his approach to actor training at the Studio in a *New York Times* article, September 2, 1956:

> The methods of the Studio derive from the work of Stanislavski and his pupil Vakhtangov with modifications based upon the work of the Group Theatre and the other work since then. . . . The simplest examples of Stanislavski's ideas are actors such as Gary Cooper, John Wayne, and Spencer Tracy. They try not to act but to be themselves, to respond or react. They refuse to say or do anything they feel not to be constant with their own characters. [28]

In the 1950s many teachers of acting viewed formal voice training for the actor as not only unnecessary, but undesirable. This rejection of voice and speech training for the American actor was influenced by a number of factors: the growing body of ethnic and regional American plays for which the Transatlantic dialect was no longer appropriate, the predominance of the "Method" approach to actor training, and the emergence of film and television as the dominant forms of popular entertainment.

The approach to voice and speech training for the actor in America's drama schools during the 1920s, '30s, and 40s had placed heavy emphasis on speech—specifically, the acquisition of Transatlantic or Theatre Speech. But the works of playwrights such as Clifford Odets, Sidney Kingsley, William Saroyan, John Steinbeck, Carson McCullers, Arthur Miller, and Tennessee Williams dealt with common men and women, not society's elite. Their plays revealed the pluralistic and multidialectic nature of America; a society deeply rooted in the ideals of democracy. The Transatlantic dialect, with its inherent suggestion of affectation and superiority, was inappropriate for the majority of characters in these modern realistic plays.

The teachers of the American "Method" were stressing the internal, psychological, and behavioral aspects of the art of acting. In *Strasberg at the Actors Studio*, editor Robert Hethmon writes:

> All of Strasberg's work is directed toward helping the actor find the reality of character, situation, and event that lies beneath the words of the play. But the actor's imagination is never aroused if his effort remains fixed on the level of the words. Strasberg calls this "adhering to the verbal pattern."[29]

"Method" teachers tended to view voice training as principally *speech* training. As such, they regarded voice training for the actor as potentially harmful to the expression of true character emotion and character revelation. But in the process of rejecting training in Theatre Speech or Standard American pronunication, many "Method" teachers and actors "threw out the baby with the bathwater," discarding not only speech training, but also the development of the vocal instrument itself. They failed to understand three important truths regarding the actor's voice. First, that the plays of American realism, and indeed every genre, require the actor to speak the play's language utilizing a mode of speech that accurately reflects the character's regional, ethnic, racial, and socioeconomic background. This challenge requires *more* technical training, not less, if the actor is to have range and casting flexibility. Second, that the theatre is *not* a democracy where the actor can impose his own regionalisms and speech patterns on every character he plays any more than he can employ his own manner of movement and wear his own clothes for each role he portrays to suffice as the character's outer means of expression. Pirandello brilliantly demonstrates this to us in his play *Six Characters In Search of an Author*, where the character of the Stepdaughter fights to have herself truthfully interpreted and presented on the stage, despite the actors' approach to their craft and the trappings of the realistic theatre. And, third, the theatre is *not* real life. The theatre is larger than life, and, as such, it requires enormous technical skill on the part of the actor to sound "natural" under highly unnatural circumstances.

By embracing the idea that an actor's performance style would appear more "natural" and "truthful" if that actor refrained from any kind of voice and speech training, the adherents of "non-training" simply denied the skills necessary for the actor to perform effectively in the theatre and opened wide the doors to the insidious practice of typecasting; a tradition that degrades and stifles the development of the actor as a creative artist. Actors were cast *because* of their vocal eccentricities, not in spite of them. And, as is still the case today, some actors were "rewarded" for vocal qualities that, in many cases, emanated from vocal misuse and abuse; huskiness and breathiness being prime examples.

Voice and speech training were replaced by the actor's use of vocal "tricks" in performance. Mumbling, throwing away the lines, talking while chewing gum, smoking a cigarette or a cigar—these became the hallmark of "naturalistic" acting. Ill equipped for the rigorous voice and speech demands of the theatre, it is not surprising that many Method-trained actors opted to move toward careers in film and television where type casting and electronic amplification could compensate to some extent for a lack of vocal technique—a lack which poses an insurmountable barrier to artistic success in the theatre. Of course no electronic amplification can compensate for an actor's lack of articulatory clarity, effective breathing, tone placement, vocal flexibility, dialect acquisition, or the actor's ability to connect his voice with the inner thoughts and emotions of the character being portrayed.

As the most pervasive medium of public entertainment, television influenced new standards of public taste in regard to the art of acting. Television demanded that actors acquire a mode of performance that was "smaller than life." Young, aspiring actors, who grew up emulating the standards of acting and vocal production supplied by television performers, tended to be ignorant and unappreciative of the heightened technical demands and artistic versatility required of the stage actor.

Finally, the popularity of television in the 1950s contributed to a phenomenon that continues to be highly evident in today's society—a lack of listening skills in American audiences. Unlike the aurally attuned "radio generation," this new television generation was conditioned to be visually oriented. Over the years many audience members have lost their ability to consciously distinguish a good voice from a poor one and the aesthetic judgment to recognize the difference between the artful handling of language by an actor and the mere recitation of memorized dialogue.

The American Regional Theatre's Influence on Voice Training

Perhaps more than any other factor, however, it was the rise of the regional theatre movement that was to shine a spotlight on the "Method's" limitations in regard to voice and speech training for the actor. In the 1960s a growing number of regional resident theatres such as the Guthrie Theatre in Minneapolis, the Arena Stage in Washington, D.C., and the Long Wharf Theatre in New Haven sought to present plays that went beyond the scope of naturalism and realism. Along with a revived commitment to producing the classics, there was also a great interest in producing the new works of writers such as Brecht, Genet, Beckett, Ionesco, Albee, and Pinter. The ideas embodied in these plays not only dictated content, but form as well. The new forms of theatre required versatile and skilled actors capable of manifesting the playwrights' non-realistic visions. In the 1960s the limitations of non-training, resulting in a highly personalized and "naturalistic" mode of speech for the actor, became evident as regional theatre directors and producers sought to hire American actors technically qualified to handle the vocal demands of their repertory seasons. In his book *In Various Directions* (1965), Tyrone Guthrie, one of the leaders of America's regional theatre movement, wrote:

> The search by actors for the truth within themselves has now gone too far. They are in grave danger of forgetting two more objective elements of truth, which no artist should dare to ignore: First, each of us is not only himself, but a member of the human race; second, it is the duty of an artist to develop the means of communication of the truth within himself, so as to share it with fellow members of the race. The Methodists overprize the search for truth as opposed to the revelation of truth. They have neglected the means of communication.[30]

Faced with the frustration of trying to find vocally-trained American actors, some regional theatre directors attempted to hire British and Canadian actors who were better equipped to handle the demanding language of classic plays and nonrealistic genres. This tactic was curtailed, however, by the Actors' Equity Association and its strict rules regarding the hiring of foreign actors. In his *A New Theatre* (1964), Tyrone Guthrie describes the origins of his repertory theatre in Minneapolis and the challenge he faced in developing a company of American actors capable of performing the theatre's classic repertory:

> If there is going to be a systematic attempt to create a definable style, certain steps will have to be taken immediately. The first and most important of these is concerned with the technique of speech.
>
> This is, to my mind, easily the most important element of the actor's craft, as opposed to his art, and one which is much neglected in the American theatre. . . . A unified and carefully considered manner of speech is, I am convinced, the first step towards evolving a distinctive acting style. It may also, just possibly, be a valuable step in the direction of an attitude towards speech, more sensible than the inverted snobbery of being reluctant to speak better than the neighbors—keeping back with the Joneses.[31]

To lead the task of voice and speech training within his theatre's first acting company, Tyrone Guthrie selected two American actors from the company to instruct and guide the other actors in finding "a unified, dignified but not pompous diction and pronunciation which is neither pseudo-British or 'Mid-Atlantic'; which is unmistakably American, will avoid the naiveté and vulgarity of much colloquial American speech, and also avoid the least attractive stigmata of English as [it is spoken] in the upper Midwest— notably an excessively nasal placement and whining drawl."[32] Guthrie explained that he decided to utilize the vocal expertise of two company members rather than a speech teacher because of the difficulty he had in finding a distinguished authority in the field of theatre speech, and "the very few whom we believe to be first-rate are engaged elsewhere."[33]

The regional theatre movement thus created an enormous need for actors with highly trained vocal instruments and teachers to train them. The times demanded the presence of someone in the field of voice for the theatre who was sensitive to the needs of American actors and capable of bringing renewed interest and respect for the voice as an inherent part of the actor's artistic expression. That someone was Kristin Linklater.

A native of Edinburgh, Scotland, Kristin Linklater became a repertory theatre actress in Scotland after completing her studies at the London Academy of Dramatic Art. In 1956, at the request of Michael MacOwen, she returned to LAMDA to assist and to teacher-train under the famed British voice teacher Iris Warren.

As head of LAMDA's voice department, Iris Warren employed an approach to voice training for the actor that was aimed at releasing, through relaxation, the actor's natural voice. According to Kristin Linklater, Iris Warren's exercises worked "from the inside out rather than the outside in. So instead of developing a musical instrument which you play, you discover your voice as a human instrument subject to the impulses of human feeling and thought. You are undoing the defenses and inhibitions which block the human channel of communication. That was her major contribution."[34]

At the urgings of her American students at LAMDA, Ms. Linklater came to the United States in October 1963 to set up a private voice studio. Describing the eagerness with which the regional theatres sought out her expertise when she first came to America, Linklater relates:

> The day after I arrived I got a call from the Lincoln Center Repertory; they were looking for a teacher. So I started working with them. That was in the Kazan/Whitehead days . . .

When the regional repertory system suddenly came into being in the early '60s there was this desperate search for teachers. They brought in voice teachers but they were teaching elocution and speech. It wasn't very organic; it wasn't linked to the emotional or imaginative and creative exploration that had been the American actor's way of working since the Group Theatre and the Actor's Studio. So, for me it was like falling into a vacuum. I was in demand. The spring after I arrived I spent three or four weeks at Stratford, Ontario, then five or six weeks at the Guthrie, and I was working at Lincoln Center, and I had my own studio in New York.

In 1965 the Arena Stage wanted me to go there, the Alley Theatre, Houston wanted me to go there, and other places were clamoring, so I realized I had to start training more teachers. Peter Zeisler at the Guthrie got the Rockefeller Foundation to fund a teacher-training program. We got sacks full of letters from people wanting to do it, interviewed about 150 people and chose twelve for a one-year program.[35]

Seven of Linklater's students finished the year-long course, and all seven were subsequently employed in regional theatres both in the United States and Canada. Among the seven was Fran Bennett who went on to serve as voice and movement director at the Guthrie Theatre for the next twelve years. Her work at the Guthrie is historically significant, not only because of the unprecedented length of her residency, but because time and circumstances allowed her to fully explore and develop the identity and responsibilities of the voice and movement director as a permanent position within a regional repertory theatre. The following is an edited transcript of my conversation with Ms. Bennett which took place on December 3, 1989:

Describe the nature of your work with Kristin Linklater in her first U.S. teacher training program.

The training encompassed a year's time, seven days a week from ten o'clock in the morning until midnight. We trained our own voices and bodies, worked with an Alexander teacher and a text teacher. We went to theatre and films together, listened to voices together, and studied vocal anatomy with the renowned otolaryngologist Dr. Wilbur Gould. We worked with some of the actors in *Marat Sade* that was being performed on Broadway at the time. Kristin had been called in to work with certain members of the company, and she brought her students along to observe and assist. The actors of this production became our "first guinea pigs" as it were. As the training progressed, Kristin secured actors from New York for her students to work with. I worked, for example, with an actor who was playing Friar Lawrence in a production of *Romeo and Juliet*. Kristin would be in attendance at these one-on-one sessions. We would work with the actors, first on their own voices and then on the text.

Around midyear there was a "weeding out" process in the training program and the number of students was reduced from twelve to seven. At the end of the year, the seven students performed in their graduation program in the presence of invited artistic and managing directors from regional theatres who were interested in having voice teachers on staff at their theatres. This was a time when theatres were very interested and desirous of having resident voice teachers as a part of their companies.

Tell me about your work at the Guthrie Theatre.

I went to the Guthrie Theatre in February of 1966. The Guthrie Theatre was then in its third year and Tyrone Guthrie was the artistic director. As voice and movement director I sat in on auditions to consult with the directors in regard to the actors' voice and movement capabilities. I taught voice and movement classes every morning and gave private voice lessons throughout the course of the day. These classes were not mandatory, but everyone took them. In fact a number of actors over the years insisted that private voice classes be written into their contracts. I led a half-hour voice and movement warm-up prior to each matinee and evening performance. Actors at the Guthrie at this time were very interested in their voices. Tony Guthrie loved voice work. Often, when I would be giving a private lesson, he would walk right in the room and participate.

I collaborated with the directors on their productions. I would observe rehearsals and would listen for those moments when something was not clear or when the actor was getting in his own way by not understanding a bit of text. Then, when I would work with that actor in a private session I would say, "Let's look at that bit of text. I'm not sure you're understanding what you're saying," or "I think you're not breathing in the right place. Let's go through that." The private text work with the actors *always* came off the rehearsals and my ongoing communication with the director.

On occasion, I worked as an assistant director. In Tyrone Guthrie's production of the *House of Atreus*, for example, I rehearsed the chorus while Guthrie was in Ireland. Then he came back and "put it all together." I collaborated with the musical directors. I worked with Stanley Silverman who did the music for *Oedipus*. He sat in on my warm-ups, and we cast the show. I would sit with him as he composed, and he would ask, "Do we have a voice to sing this?" or "Do we have a voice who can cover this sound/music?" In addition to my responsibilities as voice and movement director, I was also a member of the acting company. These were absolutely ideal times and an ideal situation for me to be working in. That's why I stayed at the Guthrie for so long.

Were all the directors and actors equally responsive to your work?

Not at all. Some of the guest directors who were brought in looked at me and my work as though I were an alien. I had to feel that out. I never had any fights with any of them. I would suggest how I could be of help to them and would invite them to visit a voice class so they could see what I was doing. After all, they had to pass my class room to get to the rehearsal room. So I would invite them in. Some directors simply didn't want to "have another body around." For those productions, I would limit my involvement to making sure that the actors were heard and understood and that the actors were always aware of the acoustical challenges involved in speaking on the Guthrie's thrust stage, where your back is always to somebody. There were actors at the Guthrie who said, "Keep your hands off me," and I would say, "Fine," and left them alone. When these actors came to me later on in the rehearsal process and asked for help, I said "Fine." I'm not suggesting that a vocal director has to compromise his or her standards for the work, but a good vocal director must have very sensitive eyes and ears to know when to say something and when not to say something to the actors and the director even when they are completely accepting of the voice work.

What do you think is the future for vocal directors in the American Theatre?

In the 1970s most of the country's regional theatres began moving away from maintaining permanent resident ensemble companies, and thus there was a decline in interest for having a resident vocal director on staff. One of the reasons the hiring of resident vocal directors has fallen off is financial. Also many directors and heads of theatres believe that voice training is now being taken care of in college and university theatre programs. I believe that interest in having vocal directors within theatres will increase as young actors, trained in professional schools and college and university programs and accustomed to working with vocal directors in the production process, enter the profession and demand to have the voice work continue. If actors entering the profession are not vocally trained and don't know how to work on a text, then *someone*—either the director or the vocal director—has to assist them. If the vocal director has been working with the director from the very beginning of the production process and knows what the director wants, then he or she can work hand in hand with the director, assisting the director in what can be a very time-consuming, but essential aspect of actor preparation.[36]

The Voice Teacher/Vocal Director
in the 1970s and 1980s

In the 1970s few regional theatre companies had the financial resources to hire a resident vocal director. The Guthrie Theatre proved to be the exception rather than the rule. Voice teachers specializing in the training of actors and unable to find employment in theatre companies turned to college and university theatre departments for employment. Kristin Linklater herself began teaching at New York University in the late 1960s.

In the early 1970s courses in voice training for the actor began to be introduced into the curriculums of college and university theatre programs. Prior to the early 1970s theatre students desiring to develop their voice and speech skills in the academic setting had to seek out voice related courses in other departments. For example, a student majoring in theatre might take phonetics in a speech department, voice and diction in a department of speech-language pathology, and singing lessons in a music department.

Along with voice teachers trained by Kristin Linklater, many college and university theatre departments hired teachers from England and voice teachers trained by the noted American voice and movement teacher Arthur Lessac. Through his work as a professional singer and his studies in speech pathology and physiology at New York University, Lessac devised a system of voice training based upon a sensory approach to voice production. His book *The Use and Training of the Human Voice*, first published in 1960 and still used today in many of America's college and university theatre departments, laid down the principles of his system. Lessac joined the faculty of the State University of New York at Binghamton in 1970 and, through the graduate program he established there and annual summer institutes throughout the country, his teachings regarding voice and movement have influenced the teaching methods of countless theatre voice and speech teachers both nationally and internationally. In 1988, Lessac said of his work:

The Lessac research and training, which is continuously in a state of work-in-progress, revolves around a sensory-awareness approach applicable to all uses of the body, with body defined in its broadest sense to include the physical, vocal, emotional, and imaginative. Our purpose and function is to train the body's voice, energy states, movement and control systems, as instruments of communication, health, resilience and perception to help illuminate the ecology of the human organism—increase human potential—reveal human talents—and promote creativity in both common and artistic endeavor.

A corollary of this is our firm commitment to the American language and American speech as an indigenous resource with its own dynamic force for effective communication and artistic expression. Our constant search for style, poetry, classic power and popular appeal can and will result in an American language and speech full of music, rhythm and instrumentation of its diverse heritage, and at the same time be clear, articulate and educated. It will reveal and provide for general, as well as specific use, a language and speech both passionate and cultured without being imitative of British culture, standards or tradition.[37]

In 1968 the Drama Division of New York's Julliard School opened under the co-directorship of John Houseman and Michel Saint-Denis. Among the first faculty members to be selected by Mr. Houseman were Elizabeth Smith to teach voice and Edith Skinner to teach speech. In his book *Final Dress*, Mr. Houseman writes:

> The first [of the faculty to be chosen] was Edith Skinner, the most highly esteemed speech teacher in America—the leading exponent, if not the originator, of so-called "mid-Atlantic" speech among American classical actors. Her reputation was enormous and her presence on our faculty brought us instant prestige.

Edith Skinner agreed to accept the position with Julliard's Voice and Speech Department on a limited basis, spending two days a week at Julliard and the remainder of the week at Carnegie Institute of Technology in Pittsburgh where, though now formally retired, she continued to teach as she had done since 1937. Throughout her long and distinguished career, Edith Skinner also served as a voice and speech coach to actors on Broadway, the Pittsburgh Playhouse, Pittsburgh's Vanguard Theatre, the Tyrone Guthrie Theatre, and the APA (Association of Producing Artists). In addition she authored the book *Speak With Distinction* (1942) and co-authored with Timothy Monich *Good Speech for the American Actor* (1981).

The priority given by Houseman to the hiring of Elizabeth Smith and Edith Skinner was no doubt influenced, not only by his own respect for the importance of voice and speech training for the actor, but by the views of his co-director Michel Saint-Denis who stated:

> The training of the voice is the most time-consuming and difficult of all our disciplines. It includes the mechanism of breathing and resonance, voice placement, articulation, diction, purity of speech, and, finally, singing—all this with a view to developing a vocal quality in the actor that is clear, rhythmic and musical. Since our aim is to achieve reality in various styles, we are not after vocal emphasis or quality for its own sake; we want the actor to have at his disposal vocal resources that will permit him to work in all styles including the most elevated.[39]

In the 1970s college and university theatre departments anxious to give an identity to their voice training programs advertised for available voice and speech positions on their faculty with wordings such as "Linklater Training Required" or "Lessac Method Only." These approaches to voice training were not always understood by the faculty involved in hiring a colleague in the field of voice and speech, but, in the absence of any degree program in the field, the voice teacher's claim to have studied the methods of one teacher or another carried a certain stamp of authority in the hiring process.

The presence of voice and speech training in college and university theatre departments throughout America in the early 1970s was greeted at best with curiosity and at worst with suspicion and total disdain. In his book *Tyrone Guthrie On Acting* (1971), Guthrie underscores this fact in the following passage:

> Too many students, by the time they achieve a degree in drama, are stuffed to the gills with theory, have imaginations which are theoretically "liberated", but which are, in fact, fettered because of their almost total lack of practical know-how, especially in the all-important field of vocal technique.

> The reason that voice-training is so neglected is that its value has been underestimated not merely by students, or by heads of drama schools, but by the general public and, in particular, by the governing bodies of schools and colleges and by ministers and ministries of education. Right now, if a particular school were to install an absolutely first-class vocal coach, the appointment would be of no general interest whatsoever. It would enhance the school's prestige rather less than the appointment of a new janitor or accountant, infinitely less than the appointment of a coach to the football team . . .

Over the next few years there will be a hue and cry for voice teachers. Since hardly anyone from the heads of drama departments down— and up—is qualified to judge whether a voice teacher does, or doesn't know his business, some strange appointments will be made. And this state of affairs will continue until, and unless, the training of "the speaking voice" once more begins to be tackled not only seriously but intelligently, until more people can tell a well-used voice from a misused voice.[40]

In the 1970s and 1980s the credibility of the voice and speech teacher in America was enhanced by the formation of a number of professional organizations of national and international scope. Two of particular importance are The Voice Foundation and VASTA (the Voice and Speech Trainers Association). Since its formation in 1969, the Voice Foundation has sponsored annual symposia on the Care of the Professional Voice designed to enhance communication between professionals concerned with the human voice; including otolaryngologists, voice scientists, speech-language pathologists, singing teachers, and teachers of voice and speech.

VASTA was formed in August of 1986. Several of the organization's stated purposes are: "(1) to encourage the development and maintenance of optimal standards in the education and training of voice and speech teachers, coaches, and consultants in theatre, film, television, communication, and video arts; (2) to develop guidelines and establish training programs for individuals wishing to become such specialists; and (3) to promote the skills of the voice and speech specialist in such a manner that he or she is recognized as being integral to the teaching of acting for the theatre, film, and television and to the development of all professional voice users."[41] VASTA's annual conferences and its association with ATHE (the American Theatre in Higher Education Association) has served to unite and provide a forum for voice and speech professionals both nationally as well as internationally.

In addition to these organizations, interdisciplinary conferences on Voice, such as that held annually at the University of Minnesota since 1980, provide an invaluable opportunity for voice professionals to share their knowledge and concerns. By bringing together voice professionals from the realms of art and science, these interdisciplinary conferences provide ideal models for college and university programs that have traditionally separated the disciplines and faculties of voice medicine, speech, singing, voice for the actor, speech-language pathology, linguistics, and psychiatry. Just as the field of Sports/Medicine has evolved in recent years to serve the needs of America's athletes, so the interdisciplinary field of Vocal Art/Science embodies the potential to serve the needs of our performing artists.

"Do You Want Me to Talk or Act?"

Since the early 1970s the idea that voice training should be an integral part of an actor's education has become increasingly accepted in America's college and university theatre programs, especially within theatre departments offering the B.F.A. or M.F.A. degree in acting. But the influence of the 1950s "Method"-oriented approach to actor training and its inherent disregard for the actor's vocal training remains strong in many educational and theatrical institutions today. Many acting teachers and directors trained in the 1950s and 1960s received no education in the discipline of voice. As a result, some acting teachers still do not perceive of voice training as being necessary for their own acting students, and many present-day directors are unaware of the fact that the actor's voice constitutes a major theatrical element in production.

This attitude among some acting teachers, directors, and the actors they work with has persisted, not only because of the influence of the "Method," but because of the unique nature of the actor's art. In the case of the dancer, singer, or instrumentalist, for example, technical expertise constitutes a significant part of the audience's aesthetic enjoyment of that artist's performance. For the actor, however, technique must be masked. The challenge of the actor to hide his technical expertise has, unfortunately, been translated by some teachers of acting and their students into the erroneous assumption that the less technical training an actor has in terms of vocal skills, the more "real" that actor will appear in performance.

In Charles Marowitz' book *Prospero's Staff*, the renowned American director and teacher of acting Robert Lewis addresses this lingering disregard for the actor's means of vocal expression in a 1985 interview with Marowitz. While chairman of the Acting Department at the Yale School of Drama, Lewis found himself working with a student on a scene from *Hamlet*. The student was corrected repeatedly by Lewis for his "New Yorky" way of talking until the student finally retorted, "What do you want me to do, talk or act?" Lewis relates that his solution to the problem was to bring "the voice and speech teachers into the rehearsals with me—so that they could actually deal with the technical problems as they were happening, not in isolation from work itself. . . . If actors work on technical things at the same time as they are working on their parts, at least they come to understand that these things belong together."[42]

The American tradition of actor training has for so many years compartmentalized the development and education of the actor that, in the process of character creation, inner thought, feeling, voice, and movement have become viewed by actors and directors as separate aspects of what should be an integral process. Lewis' comments embody the very *raison d'être* for the increasing presence of vocal directors working within the theatre today. The field of vocal direction for the theatre has evolved out of a clear and present need to assist actors within the rehearsal process to integrate what is being expressed—the language of the play—with the actor's means of expression—his voice and speech.

Notes

1. Bishop Richard Whately, *Elements of Rhetoric*, ed. Douglas Ehninger (Carbondale: Southern Illinois University Press, 1963), pp. 350–53.

2. S. S. Hamill, *The Science of Elocution* (New York: Nelson and Phillips, 1872), p. 19.

3. Dr. Samuel Silas Curry, *Province of Expression* (Boston: Expression Co., 1891), p. 45.

4. Margaret Prendergast McLean, *Good American Speech*, 3rd ed. (New York: E.P. Dutton and Company, Inc., 1952), pp. 54–55.

5. Elizabeth Reynolds Hapgood, ed., *An Actor's Handbook* (New York: Theatre Arts Books, 1963), pp. 128–29.

6. Garff B. Wilson, *A History of American Acting* (Bloomington & London: Indiana University Press, 1966), p. 283.

7. Robert H. Hethmon, ed., *Strasberg at the Actors Studio* (New York: The Viking Press, 1965), p. 283 and p. 313.

8. Tyrone Guthrie, *In Various Directions* (New York: The Macmillan Company, 1965), p. 170.

9. Kristin Linklater, *Freeing the Natural Voice* (New York: Drama Book Publishers, 1976), pp. 144–45.

10. Thomas Sheridan, *Lectures on Elocution* (London, 1762), p. 10.

11. Frederick Haberman, "English Sources of American Elocution" in *History of Speech Education in America*, ed. Karl R. Wallace (New York: Appleton-Century-Crofts, Inc., 1954), pp. 109–10.

12. Lester L. Hale, "Dr. James Rush" in *History of Speech Education in America*, ed. Karl R. Wallace (New York: Appleton-Century-Crofts, Inc., 1954), p. 233.

13. Writing about nineteenth century American theatrical traditions in their book *O'Neill*, Barbara and Arthur Gelb comment on the problems inherent in the prevailing star system: "The star, if he was so inclined, might "direct" other members of the cast, but usually he was too preoccupied with his own strategy for wringing response from the audience to pay attention to his supporting company. Rehearsals were sketchy, the star withholding

anything resembling a performance until actually playing before a paid audience. His supporting players followed suit, with the result that each performer took a stance and declaimed his big speeches oblivious to the rest of the cast. How he gestured, how he moved, how he intoned was determined by him alone. Audiences came to see their idols go through their paces—not to see ensembles interpreting a play." (See *O'Neill* by Arthur and Barbara Gelb, New York: Harper and Row, 1973, p. 28.)

14. Throughout the nineteenth century the dominant theatre artist was the actor. Until the appearance on the theatrical scene of persons such as Augustin Daly (1839–99) in the second half of the nineteenth century, there was no master director to guide actors in their interpretations, blocking, or stage business. Thus, within a given production, inconsistency of stylistic approach and interpretation were frequently present. These inconsistencies were often increased by the presence of a visiting star.

15. Wilson, p. 41.

16. Jacqueline Martin, *Voice in the Modern Theatre* (New York, N.Y.: Routledge, 1991), p. 9.

17. Steele Mackaye (1842–94), actor, teacher, and dramatist, was an important contributor to the late nineteenth century elocution movement. He introduced to America the acting theories of Francois Delsarte (1811–71). Although Mackaye successfully applied Delsarte's "science of movement" to his own acting and teaching, others turned Delsarte's theories into a set of prescribed gestures and postures that they mechanically reproduced. As a result, Delsarte's principles of expression, so acclaimed in the late nineteenth century, were rejected in the twentieth.

18. Leslie Irene Coger, *A Comparison for the Oral Interpreter of the Teaching Methods of Curry and Stanislavsky*, Ph.D. dissertation, Northwestern University's School of Speech, 1952, p. 111.

19. Giles Wilkeson Gray, "Some Teachers and the Transition to Twentieth-Century Speech Education" in *History of Speech Education in America*, ed. Karl R. Wallace (New York: Appleton-Century-Crofts, Inc.), pp. 422–24.

20. McClean, *Good American Speech*, p. 39.

21. Ibid, p. 89.

22. Ibid, p. 74.

23. Edith Skinner, *The Seven Points for Good Speech in Classic Plays* (Mill Valley, CA.: Performance Skills, 1983), p. 7.

24. Harold Clurman, *The Fervent Years* (New York: Hill and Wang, 1958), p. 31.

25. Erika Munk, ed., *Stanislavski and America* (New York: Hill and Wang, 1966), p. 150.

26. From "Broadway Dreamers: the Legacy of the Group Theatre," a television documentary presented as part of PBS television's "American Masters Series," 1989.

27. Ibid.

28. Munk, *Stanislavski and America*, pp. 159–60.

29. Hethmon, ed., *Strasberg at the Actors Studio*, p. 178.

30. Guthrie, *In Various Directions*, p. 170.

31. Tyrone Guthrie. *A New Theatre* (New York: McGraw-Hill Book Company, 1964), pp. 145–49.

32. Ibid., pp. 148–49.

33. Ibid, p. 149.

34. Susan Mason, "An Interview with Kristin Linklater," *Theatre*, Volume XVII, winter, 1985, p. 41.

35. Ibid., pp. 41–42.

36. Fran Bennett is currently a teacher of voice production at the California Institute of the Arts, a Master Voice Teacher with Shakespeare & Co., and an actress in theatre, television, and film.

37. Arthur Lessac, "Voice, Speech and Body Training by the Founder of the Lessac System," an article included in the brochure announcing the 1988 Lessac Summer Workshop in Boulder, Colorado.

38. John Houseman, *Final Dress* (New York: Simon and Schuster, Inc., 1983), p. 345.

39. Ibid.

40. Tyrone Guthrie, *Tyrone Guthrie on Acting* (New York: The Viking Press, 1971), p. 31. Used by permission of Viking Penguin, a division of Penguin Books USA, Inc.

41. From "Purposes of VASTA," published in the *VASTA Newsletter*, Volume 2, Number 3, Fall 1989, p. 6.

42. Charles Marowitz, *Prospero's Staff* (Bloomington: Indiana University Press, 1986), pp. 79–80.

Chapter 2

The Vocal Director and the Language of the Theatre

The field of vocal direction for the theatre provides a challenging and rewarding career for the individual educated in theatre and drama as well as the art and science of the speaking voice. It is a discipline that affords theatre voice specialists the opportunity to employ their knowledge of dramatic text analysis, theatre history, voice and speech production, and acting within the rehearsal process. Relative newcomers to the traditional production team, vocal directors for the theatre function as collaborative artists, serving the needs of the playwright, director, actors, designers, movement specialists, and the audience as they relate to the play's language and the vocal life of the play in performance.

A great source of inspiration and focus for the work can be taken from a passage in Robert Corrigan's *The World of the Theatre*:

> The chief function of language in the theatre is not to represent the way people actually talk in real life but to express what they experience. . . . Theatre is not lifelike—it is larger than life. This being the case, the playwright always writes in the language of his characters and not in the language of the audience. The language must be appropriate to and expressive of the characters of the play. The playwright must discover and identify with his characters and speak with their voices, rather than have them identify with him and speak in his voice. He must extract the language from the characters, not impose it on them. . . . The primary function of language in the theatre is to express the consciousness of the characters which makes their decisions to act dramatically meaningful.[1]

The very heart of the vocal director's work in theatrical production is embodied in this eloquent description of the function of language in the theatre, for it is the challenge and responsibility of the vocal director, in collaboration with the entire production team, to assist the play's director and the acting company in making certain that the language of the play serves its critical function in performance. In doing so, the vocal director helps insure that the consciousness of each of the play's characters is clearly and effectively conveyed by means of the actors' voices to the ears, hearts, and minds of the audience.

In the theatre the term characterization refers to the actor's creation of another human being, as seen by the playwright, for the stage. In the rehearsal process the actor's task is twofold, consisting of the actor's work on himself and the actor's work on his role. It is the function of the vocal director to serve the actor's vocal needs on both levels. To do so, the vocal director must not only be a collaborative artist participating in the production process, but also a highly experienced teacher of voice and speech for the actor.

Language in the Theatre

The work of the vocal director begins with text analysis; first, to study the language of the play and, secondly, to determine the major voice and speech challenges that the play's language will present in production.

Language in dramatic literature takes the form of character dialogue. The language of the characters written by the playwright and physically manifested by the voice and speech of the actors serves many important functions in production: it reveals the world of the play, provides exposition and tells the story, defines the characters and their relationships to one another, and contributes to the overall aural impact of the play in performance.

The language of the theatre takes various forms. For example, it may be written in verse or prose. It may be heightened language rich with imagery, similes, and metaphors or naturalistic and unadorned. No matter what kind of language is utilized in a given play, however, it is important to keep in mind that each word and structural combination of words has been carefully selected and arranged by the playwright to achieve a desired effect in performance. We must never lose sight of the fact that plays are written to be acted on the stage. The playwright writes the play's action and dialogue with the actors and the audience in mind.

The audience brings to the theatre certain expectations in regard to the use of language, and playwrights take this factor into account when creating dialogue for their characters. Shakespeare, for example, freely juxtaposes prose and verse dialogue within his plays as a means of imparting to the audience information regarding the characters and their relationships to one another. Dialogue written in verse, for example, may be utilized to reveal a character of nobility or a common character engaged in the expression of elevated thought and feeling. Similarly, Shakespeare's use of prose dialogue may denote that the character is of common origin or that a character of high social position is engaged in prosaic thought or informal conversation. The actor must always consider what Shakespeare's use of prose or verse means in terms of the character at each moment in the play. As John Barton points out in his book *Playing Shakespeare*, Othello's reversal from verse speaking to prose and Iago's reversal from prose speaking to verse in Act IV, scene i of *Othello* reveals Othello's mental and physical breakdown and Iago's triumph. The juxtaposition of prose and verse within this scene vividly serves to define the characters and their relationships to one another.[2]

In *Hamlet*, Hamlet's vacillation between verse and prose throughout the play provides an effective device for revealing the character's mood changes and attitudes toward those around him. When the prose-speaking Bottom in Shakespeare's *A Midsummer Night's Dream* begins spouting floral language in the "play within the play" the mode of speaking is so incongruent with the character's normal mode of speech, that his heightened language becomes a comic device.

How Language Reveals the World of the Play

The kind of language that predominates throughout a play serves to define the world of that play. Of course, there are many plays in which the characters do not speak the same kind of language. In *A Midsummer Night's Dream*, for example, Shakespeare utilizes three kinds of language to distinguish between the worlds of the fairies, the mechanicals, and the mortals. In O'Neill's *The Hairy Ape* the contrast between the formal language of Mildred and her Aunt and the common vernacular of Yank and the men in the stokehole serves to heighten the tension between the social classes within the play and their two distinctive worlds.

In addition to the use of elevated or naturalistic language, the playwright may elect to utilize regional or ethnic dialects or vernacular to establish the world of the play in terms of place, culture, and era, as well as social and educational milieu. The opening dialogue of Synge's *The Playboy of the Western World* quickly establishes, through the use of rhythm and idiom, the peasant world of the Aran islanders who inhabit the play:

PEGEEN. (*Slowly as she writes.*) Six yards of stuff for to make a yellow gown. A pair of lace boots with lengthy heels on them and brassy eyes. A hat suited for a wedding day. A fine tooth comb. To be sent with three barrels of porter in Jimmy Farrell's creel cart on the evening of the coming Fair to Mister Michael James Flaherty.[3]

Or note how, through the language, Noel Coward rapidly takes us into the world of the upper class, sophisticated, and eccentric Bliss family in the opening moments of *Hay Fever*, Act I, scene i;

SOREL. Listen to this, Simon. (*She reads.*)

"*Love's a Trollop stained with wine,*
  Clawing at the breasts of Adolescence,
  Nuzzling, tearing, shrieking, beating—
  God, why were we fashioned so!"

SIMON. The poor girl's potty!

SOREL. I wish she hadn't sent me the beastly book. I must say something nice about it.

SIMON. The binding's very dashing.

SOREL. She used to be such fun before she married that gloomy little man.

SIMON. She was always a fierce poseuse. It's so silly of people to try and cultivate the artistic temperament. *Au fond* she's just a normal, bouncing Englishwoman.[4]

Language As Exposition

The term exposition refers to the background information that the playwright incorporates into the dialogue to insure that the audience will understand the play's characters and their actions in the present. To relate pertinent information about the past while moving the action of the play forward is one of the playwright's major challenges. In his play *The Real Inspector Hound*, Tom Stoppard provides a delightful parody of bad expository writing through the character of the maid, Mrs. Drudge:

MRS. DRUDGE. (*into phone*): Hello, the drawing room of Lady Muldoon's country residence one morning in early spring? . . . Hello!—the draw—Who? Who did you wish to speak to? I'm afraid there is no one of that name here, this is all very mysterious and I'm sure it's leading up to something, I hope nothing is amiss

for we, that is Lady Muldoon and her houseguests, are here cut off
from the world, including Magnus, the wheelchair-ridden half
brother of her ladyship's husband Lord Albert Muldoon who ten
years ago went out for a walk on the cliffs and was never seen
again—and all alone, for they had no children. . . . Should a
stranger enter our midst, which I very much doubt, I will tell him
you called. Goodbye.[5]

Because a playwright's exposition is rarely as blatant as Stoppard's parody, identifying the play's exposition becomes an important part of the vocal
director's initial text analysis. Exposition may be revealed by a single word
or phrase or may be manifested within an extended monologue. Whatever
form it takes, the play's expository language will require special vocal attention by the actors in performance to insure that the story of the play is always
clear to the audience. Throughout the rehearsal process, the vocal director
keeps the actors aware of the important function of the text's exposition in
telling the story of the play and assists the actors in making certain that all
background information is vocally highlighted and clearly conveyed in performance.

How Language Reveals Character

For the playwright, dialogue represents a major characterization device
for both individual characters and groups of characters. In the theatre, the
audience learns about the characters through the way they move, the words
they speak, as well as the way they speak them. Note the following monologue selection from *Romeo and Juliet*, Act III, scene ii:

JULIET. Gallop, apace, you fiery footed steeds,
            Towards Phoebus' lodging; such a waggoner
            As Phaeton would whip you to the west,
            And bring in cloudy night immediately.
            Spread thy close curtain, love-performing night,
            That runaway's eyes may wink, and Romeo
            Leap to these arms untalked of and unseen!
            Lovers can see to do their amorous rites
            By their own beauties; or, if love be blind,
            It best agrees with night. Come, civil night,
            Thou sober suited matron, all in black,
            And learn me how to lose a winning match,

Play'd for a pair of stainless maidenhoods.
Hood my unmann'd blood, bating in my cheeks,
With thy black mantle, til strange love grown bold,
Think true love acted simple modesty.
Come night; come, Romeo; come, thou day in night,
For thou wilt lie upon the wings of night,
Whiter than new snow upon a raven's back.
Come, gentle night, come, loving, black-brow'd
night,
Give me my Romeo; and, when he shall die,
Take him and cut him out in little stars,
And he will make the face of heaven so fine
That all the world will be in love with night
And pay no worship to the garish sun.
Oh, I have bought the mansion of a love,
But not possess'd it, and, though I am sold,
Not yet enjoy'd. So tedious is this day
As is the night before some festival
To an impatient child that hath new robes
And may not wear them. O, here comes my nurse,
And she brings news; and every tongue that speaks
But Romeo's name speaks heavenly eloquence.[6]

Juliet's speech is laden with clues regarding her character at this particular moment in the play. First of all, we note that the language is written in verse and embodies many other features of heightened language; use of metaphor, analogies, alliteration, personification, and vivid imagery. The way in which Juliet speaks tells us that she is of the upper class, educated, articulate, highly romantic, imaginative, and creative. From what she says we discern that she is alone, schooled in Greek mythology, impatient, and involved in a secret romance. She knows of sex between men and women, but is herself a virgin and believes Romeo to be one also. Her face is red with excitement. Though feeling somewhat shy and timid, she is ready to give herself physically to Romeo, knowing that their love will make all things right. She adores Romeo and proclaims that he surpasses nature's wonders. Although Romeo and she have verbally promised themselves in love to one another, they have not consumated their relationship. She is as impatient as a child for the nurse to bring her news. She sees her nurse coming and anticipates an exalted report of her beloved Romeo.

In the theatre, language is character. There exists a direct connection between the words a character speaks and the character's inner consciousness from which those words emanate. Even when a character is telling a lie, the words he chooses to convey the lie and the manner in which he utters them serve to reveal the inner truth of the character at that moment in the play.

To realize how powerful a device language is in the revelation of character, one need only look at some of the first entrance lines of characters in dramatic literature to see how quickly the character's language provides us with an image of who they are. For example, the alcoholic Claire in Albee's *A Delicate Balance*: "Do I breathe gin?" and the raucous Martha in his *Who's Afraid of Virginia Woolf?*: "Jesus H. Christ . . . ," the bitter and self-pitying Beatrice in Zindel's *The Effect of Gamma Rays on Man-in-the-Moon Marigolds: (Telephone rings.)* "Will somebody get that please? *(Phone continues to ring.)* Aaaa! No help! Never any help!," the sexually confident Stanley in Williams' *A Streetcar Named Desire*: "Hey, there! Stella, Baby!" Consider Hamlet's first line in Act I, scene ii of Shakespeare's tragedy spoken in response to King Claudius' "But now, my cousin Hamlet, and my son,—" to which Hamlet utters the aside, "A little more than kin, and less than kind." Hamlet's first line not only reveals the anger and sarcasm of a quick-witted individual, but also reveals Hamlet's relationship to Claudius, thereby demonstrating another important way in which language serves the playwright.

Language As a Device to Define Character Relationships

The language of the characters defines their relationships to one another. The words a character speaks and the way he speaks them while talking to one character in a play may be completely different from the mode of speech he uses when talking to another character in the play. This difference not only helps define relationships for the listening audience, but also serves to reveal the many sides of a character's personality. In Moss Hart's and George S. Kaufman's *The Man Who Came to Dinner,* the character of Sheridan Whiteside is confined to a wheel chair for the majority of the play. This fact places major limitations upon the actor's ability to physicalize the character's multifaceted personality and his ever changing attitudes toward the many people with whom he interacts. To convey the character's chameleon-like nature and to define his relationships with other characters in the play, the actor playing Whiteside must rely on the playwright's language and his own vocal flexibility and word coloration skills.

Sheridan Whiteside, a famous theatre and literary critic, is a character who defines the identity and worth of other characters in the play in accordance with his own values and perception of reality. Upon first being introduced to Mr. and Mrs. Stanley, Mrs. McCutcheon, and Mrs. Dexter, Whiteside's response is, "I may vomit." He summarizes his attitude toward his nurse Miss Preen by saying to her: "My great-aunt Jennifer ate a whole box of candy every day of her life. She lived to be a hundred and two, and when she had been dead three days she looked better than you do now." The cook Sarah fares better in her relationship with Whiteside. He addresses her as "My Souffle Queen" who ". . . walks in beauty like the night, and in those deft hands there is the art of Michelangelo." Whiteside identifies the actress Lorraine Sheldon as "my Blossom Girl," playwright Beverly Carlton as "you Piccadilly penpusher," and his zany friend Banjo as "you mental delinquent . . . you reform school fugitive." As the actor playing Whiteside defines each of the play's characters through his use and manipulation of the play's language, the other characters, in turn, define themselves through their reactions to his appellations. Their varied responses of shock, anger, delight, joy, etc. tell us much about each character's self-image as well as the nature of their relationship with this incorrigible and fascinating man.[7]

Often a character's language will define for the audience that character's relationship with an individual or individuals who never appear on stage. Beatrice Hunsdorfer's loving description of her father in Paul Zindel's *The Effect of Gamma Rays on Man-in-the-Moon Marigolds,* Hickey's story of married life with Evelyn in Eugene O'Neill's *The Iceman Cometh,* and Levee's tortured account of his mother and father in August Wilson's *Ma Rainey's Black Bottom* are but a few examples. Note the power of language in Bernice's description of her relationship with Ludie Maxwell Freeman, a character never seen within the play, in the following passage from Carson McCullers' *The Member of the Wedding:*

BERNICE. (*squaring her shoulders*): Now I am here to tell you I was happy. There was no human woman in all the world more happy than I was in them days. And that includes everybody. You listening to me, John Henry? It includes all queens and millionaires and first ladies of the land. And I mean it includes people of all color. You hear me, Frankie? No human woman in all the world was happier than Bernice Sadie Brown.

FRANKIE. The five years you were married to Ludie.

BERNICE. From that autumn morning when I first met him on the road in front of Campbell's Filling Station until the very night he died, November, the year 1933.

FRANKIE. The very year and the very month I was born.

BERNICE. The coldest November I ever seen. Every morning there was frost and puddles were crusted with ice. The sunshine was pale yellow like it is in winter time. Sounds carried far away, and I remember a hound dog that used to howl toward sundown. And everything I seen come to me as a kind of sign.

FRANKIE. I think it is a kind of sign I was born the same year and the same month he died.

BERNICE. And it was a Thursday towards six o'clock. About this time of day. Only November. I remember I went to the passage and opened the front door. Dark was coming on; the old hound was howling far away. And I go back in the room and lay down on Ludie's bed. I lay myself down over Ludie with my arms spread out and my face on his face. And I pray that the Lord would contage my strength to him. And I ask the Lord let it be anybody, but not let it be Ludie. And I lay there and pray for a long time. Until night.

JOHN HENRY. How? (*In a higher, wailing voice*) How, Bernice?

BERNICE. That night he died. I tell you he died. Ludie! Ludie Freeman! Ludie Maxwell Freeman died! (*She hums*).[8]

To a great extent characters in dramatic literature are defined by the nature of their relationships with other characters. This includes not only past and present relationships, but also those the character anticipates having in the future. Note how, in Act I of Arthur Miller's *Death of a Salesman*, Happy's schemes for the future reveal his desire to once again have the easy success, good times, comradeship, and feeling of self-importance he experienced in his relationship with his brother Biff when the two were young:

HAPPY. (*Shouts, grabs Biff.*) Wait a minute! I got an idea. I got a feasible idea. Come here, Biff, let's talk this over now, let's talk some sense here. When I was down in Florida last time, I thought of a great idea to sell sporting goods. It just came back to me. You and I, Biff . . . we have a line, the Loman Line. We train a couple of weeks, and put on a couple of exhibitions, see?

WILLY. (*To Linda.*) That's an idea!

HAPPY. Wait! We form two basketball teams, see? Two water polo teams. We play each other. It's a million dollars' worth of publicity. Two brothers, see? The Loman Brothers . . . Displays in the Royal Palms . . . all the hotels. And banners over the ring and the basketball court—Loman Brothers. Baby, we could sell sporting goods!

WILLY. That is a one-million-dollar idea!

LINDA. Marvelous . . .

BIFF. I'm in great shape as far as that's concerned.

HAPPY. And the beauty of it is, Biff . . . it wouldn't be like a business . . . we'd be out playin' ball again . . .

BIFF. (Enthused.) Yeah, that's . . .

WILLY. Million-dollar . . .

HAPPY. And you wouldn't get fed up with it, Biff, it'd be the family again, there'd be the old honor, and comradeship, and if you wanted to go off for a swim or somethin', well, you'd do it! Without some smart cooky gettin' up ahead of you!

WILLY. (*Crosses to above table. Biff crosses to R. of Happy.*) Lick the world! You guys together could absolutely lick the civilized world.[9]

Punctuation: The Playwright's Orchestration of the Language

In analyzing a play's language the vocal director pays close attention to the playwright's use of punctuation, for it is through the use of periods, commas, semi-colons, exclamation and question marks, ellipses and dashes, parentheses, and quotation marks as well as the use of italics and capital letters that the playwright orchestrates the dialogue and provides directions for the actor regarding how the words are to be spoken in performance. This is the case for plays written in prose as much as it is for those written in verse. Note, for example, the ways in which Albee utilizes punctuation and capital letters to orchestrate the builds, intensity levels, and rhythms of the following passage from Act II of *Who's Afraid of Virginia Woolf?*:

GEORGE. (*Advancing on her.*) You will not say this!

NICK. (*Sensing the danger.*) Hey.

MARTHA. The hell I won't. Keep away from me, you bastard! (Backs off a little . . . uses George's voice again.) No, Sir, this isn't a novel at all . . . this is the truth . . . this really happened. . . . TO ME!

GEORGE. (*on her.*) I'LL KILL YOU! (Grabs her by throat. They struggle.)

NICK. HEY! (*Comes between them.*)

HONEY. (*Wildly.*) VIOLENCE! VIOLENCE! (*George, Martha, and Nick struggle . . . yells, etc.*)

MARTHA. IT HAPPENED! TO ME! TO ME!

GEORGE. YOU SATANIC BITCH!

NICK. STOP THAT! STOP THAT!

HONEY. VIOLENCE! VIOLENCE! (*The other three struggle. George's hands are on Martha's throat. Nick grabs him, tears him from Martha, throws him on the floor. George, on the floor, Nick over him, Martha to one side, her hand on her throat.*)

NICK. That's enough now!

HONEY. (*Disappointment in her voice.*) Oh . . . oh . . . oh. . . . (*George drags himself into a chair. He is hurt, but it is more a profound humiliation than a physical injury.*)

GEORGE. (*They watch him . . . a pause. . . .*) All right . . . all right . . . very quiet now . . . we will all be . . . very quiet.

MARTHA. (*Softly, with a sow shaking of her head.*) Murderer. Mur . . . der . . . er.

NICK. (*Softly to Martha.*) O.K. now . . . that's enough. (*A brief silence. They all move around a little, self-consciously, like wrestlers flexing after the fall.*)

GEORGE. (*Composure seemingly recovered, but there is a great nervous intensity.*) Well! That's one game. What shall we do now, huh? (*Martha and Nick laugh nervously.*) Oh come on . . . let's think of something else. We've played Humiliate the Host . . . we've gone through that one . . . what shall we do now?

NICK. Aw . . . look. . . .

GEORGE. AW LOOK! (*Whines it.*) Awww . . . looooook. (*Alert*) I mean, come on! We must know other games, college-type types like us . . . that can't be the . . . limit of our vocabulary, can it?

NICK. I think maybe. . . .

GEORGE. Let's see now . . . what else can we do? There are other games. How about . . . how about . . . Hump the Hostess? HUNH?? How about that? How about Hump the Hostess? (*To Nick.*) You wanna play that one? You wanna play Hump the Hostess? HUNH? HUNH?[10]

Word Repetition As a Dramatic Device

The preceding passage from *Who's Afraid of Virginia Woolf?* not only illustrates the use of punctuation and capital letters as a means by which the playwright orchestrates the language, but also Albee's use of word and phrase repetition as a dramatic device to reveal character and character relationships: Honey's witless abandon on "Violence! Violence!" and childlike, "Oh . . . oh . . . oh. . . ;" George's attempt to regain control with, "All right . . . all right . . . very quiet now . . . we will all be . . . very quiet;" Martha's refusal to give up the assault: "Murderer. Mur . . . der . . . er;" George's sarcastic mocking of Nick: "AW LOOK! Aww . . . looooook;" George's struggle to gather his thoughts: "How about . . . how about. . . ;" Note how George's repetition of the phrase "Hump the Hostess" and "Hunh? Hunh?" are used by Albee to reveal the character's obsession with the thought that his wife has been unfaithful to him with Nick. Observe also how George echoes the alliteration of "Humiliate the Host" with "Hump the Hostess" thereby demonstrating his capacity for word play and biting sarcasm as he repeats the phrase again and again to insult Martha and accuse Nick.

For the actor, word and phrase repetitions become important clues for understanding a character's inner consciousness and that character's relationships with others in the play. In the rehearsal process, the vocal director keeps the actors aware of instances of word repetition in the text and helps the actors understand their important dramatic effect and function. Dramatic literature abounds with examples of their usage. Mark Antony's repetition of the word "honourable" in his famous "Friends, Romans, countrymen" speech in Act II, scene ii of Shakespeare's *Julius Caesar* reveals the character's bold attempt to publicly insinuate the guilt of Brutus and the other conspirators under the guise of praise. Hector's repetitious use of words and phrases in Mastrosimone's *Tamer of Horses* reveals a young man frustrated in his attempts at self-expression due to his lack of formal education and his limited street vocabulary. The perfunctory question "What do you feel like doing tonight?" thrown back and forth by Marty and his friend Angie in Paddy Chayefsky's *Marty* reveals the characters' futile attempts to break free from their own intertia and customary routines. And then there is Celia's expression of ultimate joy and amazement in Act III, scene ii of Shakespeare's *As You Like It*: "O wonderful, wonderful, and most wonderful wonderful! and yet again wonderful, and after that, out of all whooping!"

Structural Analysis

A play is a thing that is made and, as such, can be analyzed in terms of its composition and structure. In his *Poetics* (425 B.C), Aristotle described the compositional elements of tragedy as being plot, character, theme, diction, music, and spectacle. Classical tragic structure consists of the play's introduction (with its inherent exposition), point of attack, rising action, climax, falling action, and the denoument or resolution. Of course there are many plays which deviate from this classical structure. The non-representational theatre of the absurdist and surrealistic playwrights are but two such examples. But basically all plays can be analyzed as either adhering to or deviating from this traditional pattern of dramatic form.

Just as a classically structured play has a beginning, a middle, and an end, so do the play's individual scenes, set speeches, and soliloquies. As John Barton explains in *Playing Shakespeare*, "Most set speeches break into three. They pick up something in the immediate situation and respond to it, they then explore the situation which makes up the bulk of the speech, and they then resolve what's been explored and either come to some conclusion or perhaps decide that there is no conclusion."[11] For example, observe the three-part structure of Titania's speech to Oberon from Act II, scene i of Shakespeare's *A Midsummer Night's Dream* in which Titania voices her position regarding the changeling boy, elaborates upon her relationship with his mother, and then reasserts her decision to keep the boy.

OBERON. . . . Why should Titania cross her Oberon?
I do but beg a little changeling boy
To be my henchman.

[BEGINNING]

TITANIA. Set your heart at rest.
The fairyland buys not the child of me.

[MIDDLE]

His mother was a vot'ress of my order;
And in the spiced Indian air, by night,
Full often hath she gossiped by my side,
And sat with me on Neptune's yellow sands,
Marking the embarked traders on the flood;
When we have laughed to see the sails conceive
And grow big-bellied with the wanton wind;
Which she, with pretty and with swimming gait
Following (her womb then rich with my young squire)
Would imitate, and sail upon the land
To fetch me trifles, and return again,
As from a voyage, rich with merchandise.
But she, being mortal, of that boy did die,

[END]

And for her sake do I rear up her boy,
And for her sake I will not part with him.[12]

It is through an initial analysis of the play's language that the vocal director becomes familiar with the world of the play, the story being told, the characters and their relationships to one another, how the playwright wants the words phrased and spoken, and how the play's events have been structurally organized by the playwright. This study of the play's language is a critical first step for the vocal director as well as for the director, actors, and designers for "the play's the thing;" the blueprint for production that gives focus to all their efforts and artistry.

Notes

1. Robert Corrigan, *The World of the Theatre* (Glenview, Illinois: Scott, Foresman and Company, 1979), pp. 194–95.

2. John Barton, *Playing Shakespeare* (London and New York: Methuen, 1984), pp. 76–77.

3. John M. Synge, *The Complete Plays of John M. Synge* (New York: Vintage Books, 1960), p. 7.

4. Noel Coward, *Hay Fever* (New York: Samuel French, Inc., 1954), p. 5.

5. Tom Stoppard, *The Real Inspector Hound* (London: Faber and Faber, 1968), pp. 15–16.

6. William Shakespeare's *Romeo and Juliet*, in *The Complete Plays and Poems of William Shakespeare*, ed. by William Allan Neilson and Charles Jarvis Hill (Cambridge, Massachusetts: Houghton Mifflin Company, 1942), p. 995.

7. Moss Hart and George S. Kaufman, *The Man Who Came to Dinner*, in *Sixteen Famous American Plays*, ed. by Bennett Cerf and Van H. Cartmell (New York: Garden City Publishing Co., Inc., 1941).

8. Carson McCullers, *The Member of the Wedding* (New York: New Directions Books, 1951), pp. 74–75.

9. Arthur Miller, *Death of a Salesman* (New York: Dramatists Play Service, Inc., 1980) pp. 46–47.

10. Edward Albee, *Who's Afraid of Virginia Woolf?* (New York: Dramatists Play Service, Inc., 1962), pp. 65–66.

11. John Barton, *Playing Shakespeare* (London and New York: Methuen, 1984), p. 88.

12. William Shakespeare, *A Midsummer Night's Dream* (New York: Simon and Schuster, Inc., 1958), p. 19.

Chapter 3

The Great White Hope:
A Model for Text Analysis

The second phase of text analysis for the vocal director involves iden-tification of the special voice and speech challenges that the play's language will present in production. Howard Sackler's *The Great White Hope* represents for the vocal director an excellent model for text analysis because it affords the opportunity to discuss a wide range of voice and speech challenges within the context of a single play.

Sackler's three-act play is epic in proportion, embodying over one hundred characters and nineteen scenes. The action of Act I takes place in various locales within the United States. The action of Act II is set in Eng-land, France, Germany, and Hungary. And, the action of Act III is played out in Mexico, the United States, and Cuba. The dialect challenges for the actors are great, involving varieties of African American and white American dialects, Standard British, Cockney, German, Hungarian, and Mexican. The stakes are high for the characters in every scene of the play, and the characters pursue their objectives with energy and a sense of urgency. The action of the play is fast-moving and visceral in nature. The actors' voices, as well as the music and sound effects embodied within each scene, play a crucial role in creating the visceral impact of the play in performance.

The Great White Hope was first produced on Broadway in 1968 with James Earl Jones in the role of Jack Jefferson. The play was highly acclaimed, winning both the Tony and New York Drama Critics Awards as well as the Pulitzer Prize. Sackler's play is a fictionalized account of the life and boxing career of Jack Johnson (1876–1946), the first black heavyweight champion of the world. The plot is loosely based upon the real-life story of the famous boxer from his 1908 victory over Tommy Burns in Sidney, Australia to his loss of the heavyweight crown in 1915 to Jess Willard in Havana, Cuba. Johnson's victory over Burns seriously threatened the racist myth of white superiority. His exuberance, strong sense of self, flamboyant lifestyle, and open relationships with white women represented an affront to the white society of his day.

Sackler's play is a powerful and brutal account of the white supremacists' relentless efforts to dethrone and destroy this spirited individual and gifted athlete. At the height of his professional career, Jack Johnson (known as Jack Jefferson in the play) is convicted of having violated the Mann Act, an act of Congress (June 1910) prohibiting the interstate transportation of women for immoral purposes. He escapes to Europe and ultimately Mexico, only to find that he is as unwelcome abroad as he was at home. Unable to box, his financial resources dwindle as his anger and sense of alienation increase. He ultimately vents his rage upon the two white people who have been closest to him throughout his career—his manager Goldie and his girlfriend Ellie Bachman. In despair, Ellie commits suicide. His spirit nearly broken by her death, Jack agrees to fight a "fixed match" in Havana, Cuba which results in his defeat.

What follows is a scene by scene analysis of the major voice and speech challenges inherent in the *The Great White Hope*.[1] It is an example of the kind of text analysis "homework" that a vocal director does in preparation for subsequent discussions with the director, designers, and actors and their collaborative work within the rehearsal process.

ACT I
Scene i: Brady's farm.

Act I, scene i contains a great deal of exposition that is critical to the audience's understanding of the entire play. The names of the play's central characters are introduced, a description of past and present circumstances is given, and a vivid depiction of the racial climate of the time are revealed in the dialogue of eleven characters in this brief four-page scene. We learn that Jack Jefferson has beaten the top two white contenders for the heavyweight championship. Now Brady, the former white heavyweight champion, is being asked to come out of retirement to fight Jack. There is a sense of urgency underlying the scene and the majority of the scene's language takes the form of rapid fire one-liners loaded with information key to understanding the story of the play.

In addition, Act I, scene i introduces a theatrical convention employed by Sackler throughout the entire play—the use of the aside. Sackler has written all the play's asides in italics and states in the opening stage directions that all the asides are to be delivered by the actors directly to the audience. These asides come at times in the play when issues are being discussed or when one character is trying to gain the audience's support for his own personal point of view. Through the use of appropriate vocal tone (e.g. friendly, sarcastic, hostile, or conspiratorial) each actor will need to establish clearly and instantaneously a relationship with the audience when delivering the asides. *Note:* Discuss with the director how these asides are to be handled in performance. *Major vocal challenges:* (1) The actors must achieve a balance in the scene between clearly conveyed exposition on the one hand and a sense of urgency (the tension of the scene) on the other, and (2) a style for delivering the play's asides must be established.

Scene ii: San Francisco. A small gym.

This scene introduces the characters of Jack Jefferson, his black trainer Tick, his white girl friend Eleanor Bachman, and Jack's former black girlfriend Clara. Here, for the first time, the audience is introduced to the sound of the African-American dialect. For this dialect, and for all the dialects inherent within the play, Sackler utilizes a writing technique known as "eye-dialect"; that is to say, he spells the words according to how he intends the characters to pronounce them. In addition to pronunciation, Sackler's dialogue brilliantly captures the syntax, idiom, rhythms, and grammar appropriate to each of the characters.

At the start of the scene, Jack is engaged in a vigorous workout, shadow boxing under the guidance of Tick. The scene embodies important exposition regarding Jack's relationships with Ellie and Clara and his future fight with Brady. Tick utters the phrase "Lively times" which will be reechoed three times in Act I, scene iv. Jack's final line in the scene—"And don't ever call me daddy"—foreshadows the last line spoken by Ellie in Act III, scene iii— "You win, daddy." *Major vocal challenges:* (1) The actor playing Jack will need to clearly convey his lines while engaged in rigorous physical movement. (2) The actors need to highlight key expository words through use of inflection, stress, and coloration. (3) Tick's "Lively times" and Jack's final line must be vocally imprinted on the minds of the audience.

Scene iii: Reno, Nevada.

Scene iii takes place outdoors in front of an arena where the fight between Brady and Jack is to take place. The scene involves many actors, or more accurately, a number of actor choruses. There is a Fourth of July atmosphere with the sounds of band music, fireworks, and a sound track of low level crowd noises emanating from inside the arena. At the start of the scene a group of white men are gambling and singing. Brady and his entourage enter for the weigh-in amidst music and cheers from the crowd. While Brady is being weighed, Jack's entourage enters, and Jack engages in verbal banter with Brady's supporters amidst jeers and catcalls. A group of Jack's supporters enter as Brady's supporters exit into the arena. Crowd noises and music continue to be heard from inside the arena as Jack addresses his black supporters. Shortly after Jack leaves, the black men begin singing "So High, So Low, So Wide", as they too exit from the stage. In short, the scene involves a cacophony of sounds: recorded voices and music, live choruses of speaker/

singers, and the voices of the scene's principal characters—Brady, Cap'n Dan, and Jack. *Major vocal challenge:* All the dialogue and physical action in this scene will need to be carefully orchestrated so that what is happening in the scene is clearly conveyed to the audience and not lost amidst a hubbub of human and recorded sounds.

Monologue: Cap'n Dan.

After the Reno scene we have the first of five extended monologues that the playwright has interspersed throughout the play. Cap'n Dan's monologue informs the audience that Jack has won the fight, and that the white boxing world is devastated by the fact that a black man is now the Heavyweight Champion of the World. Cap'n Dan informs us that a search will be undertaken immediately to find another "White Hope" who can take the title away from Jack. In sharing with the audience what the white boxing world intends to do to rectify the "calamity" of Jack's victory, Cap'n Dan's monologue represents the play's point of attack. *Major Vocal Challenges:* Each of the play's monologues function very much like Shakespearean soliloquies and should serve to further the action of the play rather than stopping it. Even when the monologue speakers are engaged in reflection, they must still convey to the audience the impression that they are delivering the monologue to us in present time and that what they are expressing within the monologue is furthering the action of the play. Cap'n Dan's monologue will require careful orchestration in terms of breathing and phrasing, use of stress, inflection, coloration, and structural build. The actor must employ heightened vocal energy at the start of the monologue in order to "take the stage" vocally and again at the end of the monologue to give the interlude a sense of finality. Through the actor's tone of voice, the character's relationship with the audience must be clearly defined.

Scene iv: Chicago. Cafe de Champion.

This scene contains vocal challenges similar to that of Act I, scene iii. A crowd of Jack's supporters has assembled outside Jack's Cafe on Division Street in Chicago. Jack enters and introduces Ellie to the crowd, referring to her as "my fiancey". There is recorded music, dancing, cheering and a feeling of "lively times". In the middle of the scene the tension is heightened by the arrival of a group of white Salvation Army workers who are introduced into the scene by the sound of a bass drum played by one of its members. As the Salvation Army workers enter, the sound of the drum reverberates throughout the theatre. Eventually the drum is taken from the Salvation Army worker by one of Jack's supporters, and absolute pandemonium ensues: blacks and whites fight one another amidst screaming, verbal threats, and the sound of police whistles. Eventually Jack stops the fighting by beating the bass drum while calling out, "Hey, hey — . . . Order in the court, boys, order in the court!" Jack continues to talk to the crowd until peace is finally reestablished. During the course of the scene, the phrase "Lively times", first uttered by Tick in Act I, scene ii, is repeated on three different occasions by three different characters who each embue the phrase with their own connotations. *Major vocal challenges:* (1) to insure that the fight scene is carefully choreographed, both physically and vocally, to make certain that none of the actors engages in vocal misuse or abuse; (2) to be sure that the actor playing Jack has sufficient breath support and the vocal power to stop the fight and control the crowd with his voice; (3) to insure that, throughout the scene, the language of the play is not lost amidst all the cheering and fighting; and (4) that each actor who utters the phrase "Lively times" does so with appropriate stress and intonation.

Scene v: Chicago. Office of the District Attorney.

In this scene a group of irate civic leaders challenge Cameron, the District Attorney, to arrest Jack Jefferson for his personal and professional affronts to the white community. Cameron interrogates Ellie in an attempt to "get something" on Jack, but to no avail. Finally, Dixon, a federal marshal, suggests that Jack's relationship with Ellie might still be the key to his demise. He proposes that Jack might be "nailed" with violation of the Mann Act. The scene thus relates three important aspects of the story: that white America is outraged at Jack's personal and professional behavior; that Ellie is deeply in love with Jack and will defend him against all attacks; and that, in the absence of a new "White Hope," government officials at both the local and national levels are bent on bringing about Jack's downfall by any available means. *Major vocal challenges:* (1) to clearly convey important exposition, and (2) to vocally highlight the beginnings and endings of each of the scene's three units of plot action to give aural definition to the scene's structure.

Scene vi: Beau Rivage, Wisconsin. A cabin.

Scene vi begins with Jack and Ellie in bed together engaged in relaxed vocal banter and physical love play. Their time together away from the rest of the world provide the play's most quiet and intimate moments. This playful, relaxed scene is abruptly interrupted by a group of law officials who burst into the cabin and restrain and arrest Jack for violation of the Mann Act. *Major vocal challenges:* (1) that the audience hear the loving nature of Jack and Ellie's relationship, and (2) that the reasons for Jack's arrest and the threat of his impending imprisonment are clearly understood by the audience amidst the shock and chaos of the scene's final moments.

Monologue: Scipio.

This extended monologue delivered by Scipio, a black revolutionary, is the only one of the play's five monologues that is delivered directly to African-American audience members. Scipio is enraged by Jack Jefferson's journey into the white man's world and his relationship with Ellie. He challenges the black members of the audience to create their own world rather than try to make it in the white man's world. During the course of this one page monologue, Scipio hurls the word "white" at the audience thirteen times, and, time and again, he uses the word "you" as a challenge in phrases such as, "How much white *you* up to? How much *you* done took on?" *Major vocal challenge:* To orchestrate this revolutionary aria in terms of breathing and phrasing, beats, stress, inflection, coloration, and structural builds.

Scene vii: Mrs. Jefferson's House

Jack's mother and her friends await the outcome of Jack's trial. As the scene commences, Mrs. Jefferson's pastor delivers a prayer. Tick arrives and relates that Jack has been fined $20,000 and sentenced to three years in prison. Jack enters and confides to his family and friends that he plans to jump bail and escape to Canada disguised as a member of a black baseball team. Clara begins to scream, and the others sing to cover her cries as Act One ends. *Major vocal challenges:* (1) The Pastor's prayer requires fullness and authenticity of expression. (2) The singing at the end of the scene needs to build in loudness and intensity to give the act a strong sound of culmination.

ACT II

Scene i: London. The Home Office.

Jack discovers that he is regarded by British authorities as being a criminal and a fugitive from justice and is not welcome in England. *Major vocal challenge:* The actors' acquisition of Standard British and Cockney dialects.

Scene ii: Le Harve, France. A Customs Shed.

A crowd of French reporters gather to welcome and interview Klossowski, a Polish heavyweight who has come to France to fight Jack. *Major vocal challenges:* (1) All the actors speak French. (2) Although he too speaks French, we must hear that Klossowski is not of French origin.

Scene iii: Vel D'Hiver. Jack's Dressing Room.

The scene involves three distinct units: Jack's preparation to fight Klossowski; Ellie's conversation with Smitty, an American news reporter, during

Jack's offstage fight; and Jack's reentrance and hurried exit after brutally beating the Polish heavyweight. *Major vocal challenges:* (1) The Handler speaks French and the fight Promoter speaks English with a French dialect. (2) The conversation between Ellie and Smitty is underscored with recorded crowd roars that steadily increase in volume and intensity. An appropriate volume balance will need to be established between the voices of the actors and the recorded sound track. (3) The final lines of the scene impart important exposition and are delivered over loud recorded boos and catcalls while the actors are engaged in a flurry of physical activity. The scene must be carefully orchestrated in terms of dialogue execution, recorded sound, and physical action to insure that the audience clearly understands what is being said.

Scene iv: New York. Pop Weaver's Office.

Dixon, a federal agent, proposes to fight promoters Pop Weaver and Cap'n Dan that a championship fight be arranged for Jack. If Jack agrees to "throw" the fight, the government will reduce his sentence for the Mann Act charge. The men believe Jack will accept the deal because his mother is ill, and he will want to return to the United States to be with her. Dixon delivers a speech describing how large numbers of blacks are migrating from their homes in the south to cities in the north. In short, this pivotal scene embodies a great deal of important exposition about the sociological climate of America at the time and how the white boxing world is going to regain the title. *Major vocal challenge:* To relate clearly the scene's exposition that is so critical to understanding the story of the play.

Scene v: Berlin. An outdoor café.

Four German officers Indian-wrestle with Jack. While Jack and Tick drink German beer, Ragosy, an Hungarian entertainment promoter, enters and offers Jack employment in his cabaret. The German officers return bringing with them an African student who speaks to Jack in English with a broken German accent. As the two converse, we learn of Jack's growing cynicism and sense of alienation. Jack's manager Goldie enters to tell Jack of the proposed fixed fight. Angered at the prospect of being "set up", Jack tells Goldie to leave and go back to the United States without him. *Major vocal challenges:* (1) The four German officers speak German and English with a German dialect. (2) The Hungarian speaks both Hungarian and English with an Hungarian dialect. (3) In speaking English with a German accent, we must hear that the African student is not a native German speaker. (4) Jack becomes more and more intoxicated as the scene progresses, and his vocal life must reflect this fact.

Scene vi: Budapest. A cabaret.

Ragosy enters and tells the story of *Uncle Tom's Cabin* in Hungarian. Jack, Ellie, and Tick then proceed to enact the story with dialogue and song. The Hungarian audience voices its disapproval. Jack removes his Uncle Tom wig and glares at them as their cries of derision crescendo. *Major vocal challenges:* (1) Ragosy and the cabaret patrons speak Hungarian. (2) The actor playing Tick impersonates Topsy in this scene and needs to employ a high, childlike, female voice. (3) Jack's growing anger must be reflected in his singing and in the way he delivers his lines in the play within the play.

Scene vii: Belgrade: Railway station.

The distant sound of artillery is heard throughout this scene, signaling the beginning of the war in Europe. As Jack, Ellie, and Tick await the arrival of a train, Smitty rushes in to tell Jack that his mother is dying. Angry and in despair, Jack demands that Smitty go back to America and arrange for a real fight. He tells Smitty he will go to Mexico, stand on the border, and make the challenge himself by crying out, "Here I is! Here I is! Here I is!" As the sound of gunfire grows louder, the act ends. *Major vocal challenges:* (1) to clearly convey the scene's exposition while maintaining a sense of urgency, and (2) to vocally build Jack's final calls in terms of strength and passion.

ACT III

Scene i: Chicago: A Funeral Procession.

Act III begins with a funeral procession for Jack's mother. The black Congregation offers up responses to the Pastor's extensive sermon. A flurry of photoflashes from white reporters suddenly cuts off the sermon, evoking an angry tirade from Clara, Jack's black ex-girlfriend. Into this scene of heightened emotion comes Scipio who blasts the preacher and the congregation for subscribing to the white man's religion. The scene continues to build in intensity and vocal power until policemen, blowing whistles and wielding nightsticks, force the crowd to disperse. *Major vocal challenges:* (1) The actors need to vocally capture the power and authenticity of the black funeral service, (2) In order to be theatrically effective, the long sermon and the responses of the Congregation will have to begin quietly and build progressively so that the photoflashes intervene just as the service is reaching its vocal climax. (3) Clara's segment of the scene must also build progressively, but then diminish. (4) Scipio's entrance begins the third major build of the scene which culminates with police whistles and screams from the crowd as the scene ends. *Note:* This scene could easily become one long exchange of yelling and screaming if the vocal builds are not carefully orchestrated.

Scene ii: New York. Pop Weaver's Office.

This is an exposition scene in which we learn that Jack has made good on his threat to go to Mexico and hurl challenges across the border at the white supremacist boxing world. Determined to destroy Jefferson, Cap'n Dan tells the audience: ". . . we're gonna squeeze that dinge so goddam hard soon a fix is gonna look like a hayride to him!" *Major vocal challenge:* To clearly relate the scene's exposition while conveying a growing sense of urgency.

Monologue: Clara.

The stage directions specify that Clara's monologue is to be accompanied by the sound of a distant bell. The character is griefstricken and obsessed with revenge against Jack. The language of the monologue is highly abstract, projecting the idea of a warning or curse. Decisions regarding the meaning of the speech will have to be made by the director and the actress. *Major vocal challenge:* The actress must strive for clarity of meaning in her vocal delivery of the monologue.

Scene iii: Juarez. A barn.

Scene iii takes place in Mexico where Jack has set up a crude training facility in an old barn. He is assisted by Tick and a young Mexican boy who speaks both Spanish and English with a Mexican accent. Angry and in despair, Jack tells Ellie to leave him. When she refuses, the two engage in a prolonged verbal and physical argument during which their dialogue intertwines. Ellie finally acquiesces with "You win, daddy"—a line which echoes back to Jack's "And don't never call me daddy" at the end of Act I, ii. El Jeffe, a Mexican sheriff enters and speaks in both Spanish and English with a Mexican accent. Goldie and two federal agents arrive to tell Jack that, if he'll agree to throw the Havana fight, his sentence will be reduced. Two Mexicans enter carrying Ellie's mud-smeared body, and we learn that she has commited suicide by throwing herself down a well. In his grief, Jack tells the men to set up the fight. *Major vocal challenges:* (1) Mexican dialects and Spanish dialogue for El Jeffe and the Boy, (2) vocal orchestration of the fight scene between Ellie and Jack, (3) highlighting of Ellie's "You win, daddy", and (4) clear delivery of all exposition.

Monologue: Cap'n Dan.

Cap'n Dan's monologue serves as a transition between the tragic and somber tone at the end of III, iii and the beginning of the Havana fight scene in III, v. We learn that the white boxing world is pinning all its hopes on a boxer known as the Kid and that Brady, the former heavyweight champion, has been selected to referee the fight. *Major vocal challenge:* to relate the expository setup for Act III, scene v while conveying Cap'n Dan's jubilation at the prospect that the Kid—"The Great White Hope"—will recover the title.

Scene iv: A street.

Amidst the sounds of a bass drum and cheering, a group of Jack's supporters collect money to send a telegram to Jack. The brief scene begins with single voices calling out their support of Jack, then several voices join together until all of the actors are calling in unison. *Major vocal challenges:* to achieve a volume balance between the cheering and drumming and the spoken dialogue, and (2) to orchestrate vocally the scene's inherent build.

Scene v: Havana: The Entrance Gate of the Oriente Racetrack.

The play's climactic scene is frought with vocal challenges. The offstage fight between Jack and the Kid is described by an actor poised atop a ladder to the ticketless crowd below who interject interlapping commentary as follows.

> MAN ONE. Cover, Kid, turn, turn—cover, he'll cave your ribs in—(ROAR.)
>
> MAN TWO. Stop the goddam—
>
> MAN ONE. Wait, no, he's up—Oh, the nigger's right on him, he's—
>
> MAN SIX. Kid, don't let him—
>
> MAN ONE. All he's got, he's workin' like a butcher—
>
> MAN TWO. No—
>
> MAN SEVEN. He's gotta—
>
> MAN FIVE. Kid—Kid!—
>
> MAN NINE. Kid—[2]

Simultaneously, scenes are being played out at another part of the stage in which a fight promoter, federal agent, and news reporter frantically discuss the fact that Jack is not throwing the fight as he was expected to. A sound track of crowd roars from inside the arena punctuates the ebb and flow of the fight, and a bell clangs loudly to denote the beginning and ending of each round. Ultimately, Jack is knocked down, and the recorded countdown of the referee inside the stadium is simultaneously voiced by the man atop the ladder. This countdown and Jack's defeat represents the climax of the play. The white onstage fans join in frantic cheering. Band music emanates from inside the arena as Jack, Tick, and Goldie enter surrounded by Pinkerton agents and men from the Press. When one of the pressmen asks Jack why he lost the fight, Jack retorts, "He beat me, dassall. Ah juss din have it." As Jack exits, the music soars again. The Kid, severely beaten, is paraded in and then taken off atop the shoulders of exuberant fans. The music swells and the lights fade as the play ends. *Major vocal challenges:* (1) to carefully orchestrate the onstage voices in conjunction with all of the recorded music and sound effects. (2) To insure, despite the rapid fire commentary by the onstage actors, the recorded sounds, and the simultaneous staging, that the account of what is happening to Jack in the round by round boxing match is always clearly understood by the audience as this aurally complex play builds to its conclusion.

The Great White Hope, as do all plays, represents special voice and speech challenges that must be identified by the vocal director through detailed text analysis before engaging in production conferences. Initially, the vocal director should discuss these anticipated vocal problems and challenges directly with the stage director in a one-on-one conference in order to make the director aware of the extent to which the vocal director's work will necessitate an ongoing communication and interaction with other members of the production team. Indeed, a play as vocally and aurally challenging as The Great White Hope demands this interaction, especially between the vocal director, the fight director, the sound designer, and the sound engineer. By establishing an early working relationship with those members of the production team whose areas most directly relate to voice within a given play, the work of the vocal director is greatly facilitated within the rehearsal process. A thorough analysis of the script prepares the vocal director to be responsive to the stage director's vision for production and enables the vocal director to provide important insights regarding the play's vocal and aural elements as they relate to all areas of production.

Notes

1. Howard Sackler, *The Great White Hope* (New York: Samuel French, Inc., 1968).

2. Ibid., p. 123. *The Great White Hope* by Howard Sackler was originally produced by Herman Levin and directed by Edward Sherin at the Alvin Theatre in New York. The excerpt is reprinted by special permission of the Lucy Kroll Agency, 390 West End Avenue, New York, New York 10024.

Chapter 4

The Vocal Director As a Member
of the Production Team

In order to function most effectively, the vocal director should be regarded as an integral part of the production team, selected by the director at the same time that the lighting, costume, makeup, scene, sound, and movement designers are brought "on board" the production process. Like the production designers, the vocal director requires lead time to fully analyze the text, consult with the director, and prepare a systematic plan for the work aimed at addressing all of the vocal challenges that the play will present in production.

All too frequently vocal directors are not brought into the production process until midway or toward the end of the rehearsal process when "suddenly" the actors' voices present a problem for the director. If the vocal director accepts such an assignment, he is forced to function without a thorough knowledge of the play's text, the director's concept, the actors' discoveries within the rehearsal process, or the production designs. It is, to say the least, a difficult and frustrating position in which to find oneself as an artist in the theatre.

Rarely would a professional director send an actor to an unconsulted costume designer during the last week of rehearsal with the request that the costumer find "something" for that actor to wear opening night. But a theatre voice specialist is frequently confronted with this very situation when an actor seeking vocal assistance states, "My director doesn't like my voice in the play. Can you help me?" As sympathetic as the vocal director may be to the needs of the actor and the director, the only truthful response is, "No. Not until I have read and analyzed the play, consulted with your director, and heard you in action in the rehearsal process with your fellow actors in the theatre where you are to perform." It is one thing to teach an actor vocal technique in a private lesson, but when the vocal needs of that actor are related to performing in production, then the actor's voice must be heard and developed within the context of that production, not in isolation from it.

The actor's voice is a primary means by which the actor expresses a character's inner life. As such, an actor's vocal life cannot be separated from the process of character creation and that character's physical manifestation in performance.

The rehearsal period involves a conditioning process in which the actors explore and become comfortable with specific modes of physicalization, vocalization, and intellectual and emotional expression as they are appropriate to their given characters. A function of the vocal director is to assist the actors in the healthy and full expression of their characters' vocal life. In order to fulfill this function optimally, the vocal director needs to be brought in at the very beginning of the rehearsal process. If brought in late in the rehearsal process, the vocal director will most likely find that the actors have already set many aspects of their characters' vocal life. Yes, needed changes can be made, but, in many cases, the actors may feel quite comfortable with their established mode of vocal expression even when that mode of expression is abusive to their vocal instruments and ineffective in regard to character revelation. To ask an actor to make changes in his voice and speech during the final stages of character development can prove to be a very disruptive and often impossible challenge and should be avoided.

When Should a Director Seek the Assistance of a Vocal Director?

Indeed, every theatrical production can benefit from having a vocal director as a member of the production team. Even when the play's director is highly trained in the areas of voice and speech for the actor, the many demands placed upon a director during the rehearsal process severely limit the amount of time he can devote to the actors' voices and to analyzing the numerous challenges and subtleties of voicing the play's language in performance. Directors will find that collaborating with vocal directors can be especially helpful in the following instances:

1. When much of the play's action is housed within the language; that is, the play's major action is carried through the dialogue. (For example, the plays of Shakespeare and Shaw, O'Neill's *Long Day's Journey Into Night,* or Albee's *Who's Afraid of Virginia Woolf?*).
2. When the play requires that the actors' voices compete with extensive and ongoing sound effects, such as in O'Neill's *The Hairy Ape* or Peter Weiss' *Marat Sade.*
3. When the play employs heightened language; that is, language that is not naturalistic, but is rich in imagery, similes, and metaphors and may be built upon a definite rhythmic structure, such as Shakespearean verse.

4. When the play is nonrealistic and requires the actors to do extraordinary things with their voices. Three such examples are Beckett's *Waiting for Godot,* Shepard's *Tooth of Crime,* and Ionesco's *The Bald Soprano.*
5. When special character voices are required, as is the case in many plays for young audiences, in story theatre, in fanciful plays such as Shakespeare's *A MidsummerNight's Dream,* or for the stock characters of commedia dell'arte.
6. When the play requires strenuous physical action that must be coordinated with the speaking of dialogue. This includes most musicals and any play that involves stage combat and/or extensive physical movement; such as, Mastrosimone's *Extremities,* Shepard's *Fool for Love,* and Rostand's *Cyrano de Bergerac.*
7. When plays require the use of dialects and/or foreign languages.

The Director/Vocal Director Relationship

It is the responsibility of the play's director to bring unity and focus to all of the various elements of production. These elements include the script, the actors' performances, the physical staging, and the production designs. As the play's primary visionary and organizer, the director needs to establish early and ongoing communication with each member of the production team, including the vocal director. The collaboration of the vocal director and the stage director should commence with a one-on-one preproduction meeting in which the following matters are addressed.

The director should share with the vocal director his concept for the production in terms of the physical staging as well as how the language of the play is to be handled. One of the most important questions for the vocal director to ask the play's director in this initial session is, "How do you want the actors to sound within the context of your production concept?"

Having fully analyzed the text in terms of the language, the vocal director can utilize this preproduction meeting to share with the director his initial impressions regarding the vocal challenges inherent in the text as well as those suggested by the director's expressed concept for the production. The special vocal demands and challenges of each individual character as well as those for the acting company as a whole need to be identified clearly. Each character's mode of pronunciation needs to be addressed. Here the vocal director can be of assistance to the director by discussing such topics as the pros and cons of dialect usage, the distinction between Standard American and Transatlantic pronunciation, and the differences between a stage dialect versus an authentic regional, ethnic, or foreign dialect.

It is important in this initial session for the vocal director and the director to discuss the acoustical demands of the theatre in which the play is to be produced. The vocal director needs to know "up front" if the director is considering using microphones for the actors to compensate for poor acoustical conditions of the playing space or to achieve special dramatic effects with selected characters. It may be necessary for the vocal director to advise the director regarding the pros and cons of using electronic amplification in the theatre and, specifically, how such sound reinforcement will affect the nature of the production being addressed within the designated playing space. The two should discuss the vocal demands of the play in terms of the music and sound effects called for by the playwright and any additional aural elements that may be part of the director's production concept.

It is also important for the vocal director to know if the director intends to have the actors memorize their lines prior to the first rehearsal. This is not an uncommon directoral practice, but one which, in my opinion, should be avoided whenever possible for the following reasons. When an actor is asked to memorize his lines prior to the rehearsal process, the actor learns and begins to interpret those lines in isolation from the director and the other actors. Line readings, often inappropriate and inaccurate, become set in the actor's mind and voice, denying that actor the spontaneity so crucial to making the language of the play come alive in performance. Line memorization is often undertaken by the actor in a rapid fire, droning mode of utterance without any awareness of the sense of the words or the appropriate inflection required to make the dialogue clear to the listener. As a result, the vocal director and the director may have to spend a great deal of time with the actor in rehearsal helping that actor to unlearn what has become second nature to him through the memorization process.

In light of the production's vocal challenges, the director and the vocal director need to discuss what they will be listening for in the audition process. This includes numerous vocal qualifications ranging from vocal expressiveness, flexibility, and stamina to vocal quality, pitch, and articulatory clarity as they relate to the demands of the play's various characters.

Once the director has shared with the vocal director his concept for the production and how he wants the actors to sound within the context of that concept, the vocal director should provide an initial assessment of what he will need in terms of time and resources. The amount of time the vocal director will need to assist the actors in mastering the language of the play and to realize the director's concept in terms of the vocal life of production will vary according to a number of factors: the degree of difficulty of the play's language, the director's production concept, the level of voice and speech training that the actors bring to their roles, the size of the cast, the dialect requirements, and the acoustical demands of the playing space. At this stage in the production process, the vocal director can only provide a rough time estimate, for he cannot "assess the job" fully until casting has been completed and he has heard and analyzed the entire company in an initial read-through of the play. In making this initial assessment, it is sometimes helpful to ask the director, "Who has already been cast?" or "Who is being considered for casting?" The experience and amount of voice and speech training the actors bring to the production will, of course, affect the amount of time required of the vocal director.

The vocal director needs to explain clearly to the play's director how he intends to go about his work on the production. To aid the director and the stage manager in setting up a rehearsal schedule, the vocal director should alert the director to the fact that he will require one or two rehearsal sessions with the entire acting company at the start of the rehearsal period to deal with specific vocal challenges (such as dialect acquisition or instruction on how to approach the speaking of verse) and to teach a vocal warm-up.

The vocal director must stress two important points in this initial meeting with the director. *First of all, there must be an open and on-going communication between the vocal director and the director throughout the rehearsal process. Secondly, the work of the vocal director must always emanate from the rehearsal process itself.* The key to establishing effective collaboration between the vocal director, the director, and the actors is in the shared experience of the rehearsal process. Only by observing the rehearsal process on a regular basis can the vocal director and the director "think as one" in regard to their work with the actors. This "thinking as one" is critical if the vocal director, like the play's designers, is to work accurately and effectively with the actors in realizing the director's concept for production. It is important for directors to understand that, even when it may seem to them that a scheduled rehearsal has nothing to do with voice, there is always something invaluable for the vocal director to gain from attendance at a rehearsal. Rehearsals focusing on characterization, stage combat, or text interpretation, for example, all provide valuable information for the vocal director in regard to the challenges of voicing the play's language in performance. If directors understand this, they will not feel that they are taking up the vocal director's time just because the rehearsal does not involve a full run-through or the vocal director's "hands on" involvement with the actors. The vocal director, like the actors, needs to be constantly gathering information from the director and from the rehearsal experience itself. Important breakthroughs regarding text interpretation and characterization can come at any time. If the vocal director's work with the actors is undertaken separately and does not emanate directly from the rehearsal process, then breakdowns in communication between the actors, director, and vocal director can occur. Confusion can result, and incorrect assumptions regarding the director's interpretation can be made. This should never occur and need not occur if the director and the vocal director are thinking as one. Once this need to "think as one" has been agreed upon, it is helpful for the director to share this agreement between himself and the vocal director with the actors when the director initially introduces the vocal director to the acting company. This simple announcement regarding the director/vocal director relationship can go a long way toward establishing, at the outset, an atmosphere of trust between the actors and the vocal director.

Lastly, the vocal director needs to discuss with the director how vocal notes can best be conveyed to the actors during the rehearsal process. When working with a director for the first time, it is helpful to explain what kinds of written notes will be taken during the play's rehearsals and run-throughs. One may recommend that, at the first two rehearsals where the vocal director takes voice notes on several scenes or an act of the play, time be alotted at the end of the rehearsal for the vocal director to give notes orally to the acting company. By doing so, the director and actors can hear what the vocal director is listening for in regard to the play's vocal life and each actor/character in particular. These oral critiques can enhance vocal awareness within the acting company and help to build trust between the director and the vocal director. After the first few rehearsals, however, the vocal director may choose to limit oral notes at the end of rehearsal to a brief statement to the entire company, conveying more detailed individual voice notes to the actors in written form.

Preproduction Meetings with the Director and Designers

Having first met with the vocal director and the designers in one-on-one sessions, the director then brings the entire production staff together to talk about their proposed designs for the production; how the designers intend to execute their designs and what they need from one another. This meeting affords the vocal director the opportunity to share with the designers the play's vocal challenges as determined by his analysis of the text and his one-on-one discussions with the director.

As the other members of the production team share their ideas regarding their production designs, the vocal director should be alert to any information coming from the designers that relates to the actors' voices in performance. This is a very important meeting for the play's vocal director, for nearly every aspect of the production design has an impact, either directly or indirectly, upon the actor's vocal instrument and mode of vocal expression. There are a number of considerations the vocal director should take into account when listening to and consulting with the other members of the production team.

The Theatre Space and the Set Design

What is the nature of the theatre space—stage and auditorium—in which the play is to be presented? Is the theatre acoustically sound? Does the theatre have echoes or acoustical dead spots? Is the theatre a large space that will place demands upon the actors in terms of projection? Is it a small space that will require that the actors control their volume so that they don't assault the audience's ears? Is the set going to be realistic or nonrealistic? Two dimensional or three dimensional? Is it going to be lushly ornate or unadorned? What building materials are going to be used and how will they affect the acoustics of the playing space? Are there going to be any scene shifts going on while the actors are on stage speaking and, if so, what kind of sounds will the scene shifts create under the actors' voices?

The Costume Designs

What will the actors be wearing? How will the costumes be fitted? Is there anything about the design of the costumes that might be restrictive to the actors' vocal instruments? In what ways do the costume designs dictate character and, therefore, the voice that must reveal that character? Are masks to be worn? Will the masks have the mouth area cut out or covered? Are the actors' heads and faces to be covered? (For example, the ass head in Shakespeare's *A Midsummer Night's Dream* or Wolf in Sondheim and Lapine's *Into the Woods*).

The Makeup Designs

In the preproduction meeting, the vocal director should be alert to any proposed makeup designs that might have an effect upon the actors' voice and speech. Might the makeup designs cause any kind of vocal or articulatory distortion? (For example, the use of a moustache frequently requires the actor to give greater attention to his clarity of articulation. Or, the use of latex on an actor's face and neck can restrict the freedom of the actor's mouth and jaw movements, thus placing restrictions upon the actor's voice and articulation). If the makeup designs are going to distort the actor's voice and speech in any way, will the actor be able to make the adjustments necessary to be heard clearly and understood without doing damage to his vocal instrument or should the makeup design be modified to accommodate the voice and speech demands of the actor?

The Lighting Design

On the surface it may seem that there is no connection between the vocal director and the lighting designer. However, in many instances there is a very strong connection. One of the responsibilities of the lighting designer is to utilize light to create atmospheres and environments in the theatre. Atmospheres are created through color and intensity of light on the stage, and environments are created through the focus of the light, as well as the presence and the absence of light. The vocal director needs to be aware of how the presence or absence of light on the stage affects the actors' voices. Given today's visually oriented society, it is usually the case in the theatre that the dimmer the lighting the harder the audience will have to concentrate in order to hear the actors and the more actively the actors will have to articulate in order to be clearly understood by the audience. In the production meetings it can be very helpful for the vocal director to learn what kinds of atmospheres and environments are going to be created and how the lighting designer is going to create them. The actors, as characters, will be affected by these various atmospheres and environments in performance, and their effect will be reflected in the actor's vocal expression.

The Sound Design

Perhaps the vocal director's closest relationships on the production team are with the sound designer and the sound engineer. It is the responsibility of these three individuals to maintain an ongoing communication throughout the rehearsal process in order to establish a proper balance between the human and nonhuman sounds of the production, insuring that the audience can always hear the actors with ease and clarity. The preproduction meetings afford the opportunity for the director, sound designer, sound engineer, and vocal director to address a number of key issues relating to the aural elements of production. For example, if music is a part of the production design, what kind of music will be used? (Original compositions? music familiar to the audience? music with lyrics?) Will the music be utilized between scene and act breaks only or will it be used to underscore the actors' dialogue as well? At what point in the play will sound effects (e.g. rainfall, thunder, wind) be competing with the actors' voices? Will the actors be "miked" at any point in the play? Where will the speakers be set in the theatre? For example, will the sound from the speakers be emanating from the back of the auditorium?

in front of the auditorium? from the back of the stage? from an on-stage area? from multiple directions simultaneously? In each instance, the vocal director, in consultation with the sound designer and sound engineer, will need to evaluate the effects the placement of the speakers will have in regard to the actors' voices and the audience's ears. If the vocal director has a clear understanding of the sound design from the start of the rehearsal process, then he will be better able to help prepare the actors for those moments in the play that will require special vocal handling in terms of projection, clarity, and tone.

Choreography and Stage Combat

Throughout the rehearsal process the vocal director also collaborates with the choreographer and the stage combat specialist. If an actor is called upon to dance and speak at the same time, for example, then the dialogue must be carefully orchestrated for the actor in terms of breathing and phrasing to insure that the actor's voice is clear and supported at all times. Just as all stage combat sequences are carefully choreographed to prevent physical injury to the actors, the language and human sounds that accompany such moments of heightened physical activity must be carefully prepared for and rehearsed by the actor to prevent vocal injury. The more violent the physical action on the stage, the more conscious the actors must be in terms of their vocal execution in order to avoid any "vocal accidents" resulting from vocal misuse and abuse. It is, therefore, of utmost importance that the vocal director and the stage combat specialist work together with the actors and the director on all sequences of heightened physical action that also involve the actors' voices.

Stage Properties, Special Effects, and Special Considerations

During the preproduction meetings, the vocal director can serve as a consultant for the director and the other members of the production team regarding the use of stage properties or special effects as they relate to the actors' vocal instruments. For example, will the actors be required to smoke on stage or can an alternative piece of business be found? Will fog machines be utilized? If food is to be consumed on stage which may cause vocal problems, what kinds of foods might be substituted? For example, the character of 'Bo' in William Inge's *Bus Stop* is required to drink a quart of milk on stage. Dairy products can result in an overproduction of phlegm that affects the clarity of the speaking voice. Therefore, in this case, a milk carton filled with water would be a better choice than a milk bottle filled with real milk.

The main concern here is the vocal and physical health of the actors. By helping the director and production staff identify, at this pre-rehearsal stage, those substances that might prove detrimental to the actors' vocal health and effectiveness, vocal problems and needless vocal abuse in rehearsal and performance can be prevented.

The Audition Process

In the audition process the vocal director serves as a consultant to the director in terms of each actor's present and potential vocal life. In the audition process the director attempts to minimize, through optimal casting, as many potential rehearsal and production problems as possible. Actors who appear to be problematic in one way or another tend to be passed over in the audition process. The director knows that he has a limited amount of time to mount a given production and that actors with problems—be they physical, vocal, psychological, or experiential—tend to slow down and frustrate the creative process. The list that follows represents some of the factors that vocal directors listen and watch for in evaluating the actor's voice in the audition process.

1. Is the voice healthy?
2. Is the actor's physical posture optimal?
3. Is the voice properly placed and resonant or is it throaty or nasal?
4. Does the actor breathe and phrase effectively?
5. Is the actor's pitch placement optimal? And, does the actor exhibit pitch range flexibility?
6. Does the actor's voice project readily without any signs of forcing or straining?
7. Is the actor's articulation active and clear?
8. Is the actor hard to understand due to a tight jaw or lazy lip activity?
9. Is the actor employing pitch variety and inflection to illuminate the meaning of the text?
10. Is the actor's voice appropriate in terms of pitch, tone, accent, etc. for the character being cast?
11. Is the mode of pronunciation being utilized appropriate to the character in the audition piece?
12. Does the actor's voice sound natural and unmannered?
13. Are the character's thoughts and feelings being actively and effectively communicated by means of the actor's voice?

14. Is the actor open to exploring suggestions from the director or the vocal director regarding his voice and the vocal interpretation of the monologue?
15. Does the actor demonstrate a high degree of vocal flexibility in executing these vocal and/or interpretive changes?
16. Has the actor had previous voice training? If so, how much? Where and with whom did the actor study?

All casting decisions are ultimately the responsibility of the play's director. But in this difficult and often exhausting process, the vocal director represents a valuable consultant who can assist the director, as needed, in determining an actor's vocal capacity for undertaking a given role. If the director wishes to cast an actor who has obvious vocal problems, the vocal director should be able to make a realistic assessment as to whether or not the actor's vocal problems can be successfully corrected within the time limits of the rehearsal period.

The Read-through Rehearsals

Once the play has been cast, the acting company is brought together to read the play aloud. These initial read-through rehearsals provide the vocal director with an invaluable opportunity to listen to the actors as well as to continue to absorb the director's ideas regarding the play, its characters, and the production concept. In read-through rehearsals where the actors give a "straight" reading of the play and do not engage in any premature attempts at vocal characterization, the vocal director has the opportunity to hear and analyze each actor's voice and speech in terms of its strengths and weaknesses. The vocal director can then share these initial analyses with each actor in scheduled one-on-one sessions or during the voice orientation session with the acting company. These analyses will provide a helpful guide for the vocal director in selecting specific voice and speech exercises for each actor and in designing a vocal warm-up for the acting company as a whole.

The first read-through rehearsal is also an excellent time for the vocal director to share with the acting company what he, the director, and the designers have identified as being the major vocal challenges inherent in the play and describe how he intends to go about working with the actors, the director, and the designers to insure that these vocal challenges are mastered during the rehearsal process.

The Vocal Orientation Session
with the Acting Company

Scheduling a session for the acting company and the vocal director at the beginning of the rehearsal process provides an invaluable opportunity for the vocal director to address voice issues related to the production and to impart voice and speech information needed by the entire cast. For example, while many actors have had vocal training in one form or another, many others have not and have no knowledge of how the human voice is produced. It can be, therefore, very useful to incorporate into the vocal orientation session a brief talk on the vocal mechanism as well as how the actors can develop and maintain optimal vocal health and stamina throughout the rehearsal period and run of the show.

A basic vocal warm-up can be taught, discussed, and executed several times within this first orientation session. This vocal warm-up is designed by the vocal director to address the specific needs of the acting company and the play they are performing. At this time, a printed copy of the warm-up can be distributed to the acting company along with any additional information appropriate to the voice and speech needs of the production.

The voice orientation session provides an excellent opportunity to share with the acting company the notes taken by the vocal director during the read-through rehearsals. Once the actors are made aware of their individual vocal strengths and challenges, they can be given specific exercises to incorporate into their daily warm-up routines. In addition, the vocal director can discuss with the actors the vocal challenges unique to each character as well as the special considerations the actors will need to take into account while mastering the play's language; for example, punctuation, expository dialogue, word repetition, and antithetical words and phrases.

Because most voice notes in subsequent rehearsals will be conveyed to the actors in written form, the vocal director will need to familiarize the company with the terminology and symbols that will be employed in the note-giving process. For example, written notes regarding pronunciation may be conveyed to the actors by means of International Phonetic Alphabet symbols or by the system of phonetic symbols used by Arthur Lessac in his text, *The Use and Training of the Human Voice*. If the actors are not familiar with either system of notation, then one or the other will need to be taught so that the vocal director's pronunciation notes will be clearly and readily understood. To this end, it is helpful to include in the actors' handouts a vowel and consonant chart that illustrates the IPA symbol for each phoneme and/or the Lessac system of phonetic symbols. The actors can then refer to these charts as the need arises.

The voice orientation session with the actors usually takes about two hours of rehearsal time. But the early scheduling of this session will prove invaluable and timesaving "down the rehearsal period road." The vocal orientation helps insure that the entire acting company begins thinking of their voice and speech production and vocal health as being an integral part of the creation and performance of their characters. Such an awareness can go a long way toward preventing misuse and abuse of the actors' voices and thus can help minimize, if not totally prevent, actor-absenteeism in rehearsal and performance resulting from voice-related problems.

If the play requires special voice and speech demands of the entire cast, such as stage screams and other forms of heightened voicing, dialect acquisition, or speaking verse dialogue, then an additional company voice rehearsal should be scheduled so that the vocal director can instruct the entire cast simultaneously. Dialect tapes and manuals can be distributed or handouts explaining the guidelines for verse speaking can be given to the actors at this time so that each cast member can continue working on his own as well as within subsequent small group and one-on-one sessions with the vocal director.

The Rehearsal Period

If the director and the vocal director have agreed to incorporate a vocal warm-up into the rehearsal process, the vocal director or his assistant leads the acting company in a warm-up before each rehearsal. More experienced actors may prefer to do their vocal preparation on their own before coming to the theatre, but a group warm-up can serve a number of positive functions. Along with helping to insure the acting company's vocal readiness to rehearse, the group warm-up encourages a disciplined approach to the work and helps to build a sense of ensemble within the acting company. The company warm-up will be discussed in greater detail in the following chapter, but, in general, this prerehearsal/preshow warm-up should include a progressive series of exercises designed to address the actors' physical relaxation and flexibility, activation of the breathing muscles and vocal resonance, voice strengthening, pitch range flexibility, articulatory flexibility, dialect drills if required, and a physical and vocal transition into character. The warm-up needs to be disciplined and focused, make effective use of the available time, and *not* exceed the alotted time.

Along with conducting a vocal warm-up prior to each rehearsal, the vocal director's responsibilities in the early stages of the rehearsal process include: 1. observing rehearsals, 2. maintaining an ongoing communication with the director, and 3. working with the actors in one-on-one or small group sessions. *Note.* Through consultation with the stage manager and the director, these voice sessions with the actors can be scheduled at times that do not conflict with the actors' acting/staging rehearsals.

The Run-through Rehearsals

Once the production gets "on its feet," the vocal director sits in the house to serve as a listening audience of one for the scenes or acts being presented and takes notes on various aspects of each actor's vocal life, including.

Breath support.   Is the actor's breathing efficient and relaxed? Is the actor making effective use of his abdominal and intercostal muscles for optimal breath support or is the actor employing upper chest/shoulder action resulting in shallow, inefficient inhalations and a breathy tonal quality?

Coordination of breathing and phrasing.   Is the actor taking quick refill breaths at logical thought pauses, thereby making the sense of the language clear to the listener? Does the actor consistently sustain vocal tone throughout the entirety of phrases and sentences or does the voice become breathy? If the latter is the case, final words of phrases and sentences may not be heard and throat constriction will replace an open, relaxed production of vocal tone.

Vocal placement.   Is the actor's voice resonating in the oral cavity or are jaw tension and inactive lip activity (mumbling) limiting optimal mouth resonance? Is there an inappropriate use of nasal resonance? Is throat constriction prohibiting optimal resonance of the vocal tone in the pharynx?

Head, neck, and body alignment.   Does the actor's physical posture lend itself to optimal vocal tract openness and optimal breath support? Or, is poor head, neck, and body alignment resulting in problems such as constriction of the breathing muscles and vocal tract?

Articulatory clarity.   Is the actor clearly and readily understood? Are the vowel sounds full and the consonants actively sounded or is there an inactive use of the articulators resulting in unintelligible speech?

Pronunciation. Is the actor's word pronunciation (individual phoneme production, as well as the use of stress and intonation) appropriate for the character and the world of the play?

Dialect consistency. Is the actor's dialect consistent in terms of phoneme production, resonance placement, use of stress, and intonation? Is there a dialect consistency among all the actors speaking the same dialect?

Vocal highlighting of the beginnings and endings of beats, scenes, and acts. Are the actors using appropriate vocal energy at the beginnings and endings of major units of action within the play to insure that the structure of the play is aurally defined for the audience?

Appropriate use of stress and inflection to insure clarity of meaning. Is the actor making appropriate use of stress and inflection to clearly convey the meaning of the play's language and reveal the inner consciousness of the character?

Pitch placement. Is the actor initiating vocalization on an optimal pitch where volume can be produced with a minimum of effort and upward and downward inflections can be executed with ease?

Pitch variety. Is the actor employing an appropriate amount of pitch variety? Is the actor monotone or slipping into a repetitious pitch pattern that obscures the meaning of the language and bores the listener?

Instances of vocal misuse or abuse. Is the actor employing laryngeal/pharyngeal tension to increase vocal volume? Is the actor initiating vocalization at a pitch level that is too high or too low to insure easy and effective vocalization? Is the actor's voice breathy due to insufficient breath support? Is the actor's voice throaty in its tonal quality as a result of insufficient breath support, laryngeal/pharyngeal tension, or lack of energized lip activity?

Coordination of voice and speech sounds with stage movement. Is the actor's clarity of articulation being obscured in moments of heightened physicality? At such moments, does the actor need to increase breath support or take more frequent breaths to insure a solid tone? Is the actor allowing the intensity of a fight scene to result in laryngeal/pharyngeal tension?

Moments of optimal voice usage. Just as it is important to make actors aware of their voice/speech challenges throughout the rehearsal process, so is it equally important to give them feedback on what they are doing well.

In this note-taking process, the vocal director may find it helpful to use legal-size note pads, placing the character's name and the rehearsal date at the top of each page or page division. As the vocal director listens to the play, follows the text, and records the voice notes, it will prove a helpful reference for the actor if the vocal director indicates beside each note the page number where the given word or line can be found in the text. It is an important timesaving strategy for the vocal director to keep the voice notes for each character separate from all the others so that, at the end of each day's rehearsal, the individualized notes can be readily handed out to the actors.

Written voice notes are an effective way to communicate with the actors for several reasons. First of all, after every rehearsal the director and the stage manager need to give notes to the actors. Once additional theatrical elements begin to be introduced, the director and the stage manager are joined in these post-rehearsal note-giving sessions by other members of the production team—the scene, costume, lighting, makeup, and sound designers; the prop master; the choreographer and stage combat specialist. These note sessions following the acting rehearsals come at a time when the actors are tired and are ready to conclude their work for the day. Giving a brief oral comment to the entire cast regarding general vocal observations combined with providing the actors with individualized written notes works very effectively for all concerned. The actors have their voice notes in writing and the page numbers in the text to which the notes refer, and they can study the notes and the text at their leisure prior to the next day's rehearsal.

There are actors who are able to take voice notes and assimilate the needed changes in the next day's rehearsal. It is more often the case, however, that the same voice note will have to be given to an actor more than once and, in some instances, many times. Directors often face this same frustration of having to repeat a direction to an actor over and over again. The vocal director should not be disheartened by this fact, but simply continue to write the same note to the actor rehearsal after rehearsal until the required voice or articulatory adjustment is made. When the necessary adjustment is made, written or oral feedback to the actor can reinforce the breakthrough. In some instances, the actor has become "locked" into an inappropriate mode of voicing or pronunciation at an unconscious level. If the problem persists, the vocal director should make the director aware of the actor's habit so that the director can assist the actor in exploring the root of the problem. For example, the actor may be misinterpreting the character, or the actor's self may be getting in the way of the character.

As the production enters the full run-through phase, the vocal director continues to sit in the house and take notes. It is important for the vocal director to sit in various locations within the theatre auditorium during these run-throughs to insure that the actors will be clearly heard by all the audience members. Sitting in the last rows of the theatre auditorium is always a valuable way to discern audibility for the entire audience. It is also important, however, for the vocal director to experience sitting in the first rows of the theatre to be sure that the actors' voices are not too loud for those audience members who will be sitting in close proximity to the stage.

Even if an actor is skilled in monitoring the projection of his voice through the use of breath, vowel elongation, and resonance, it is impossible for him to hear his voice as others hear him. Thus the actor must receive feedback from a critical listener sitting in the auditorium. Because the bodies of the audience members will absorb some of the sound of the actors' voices in performance, the vocal director must be capable of providing the actors with as accurate an estimate as possible regarding the volume levels that will be necessary to fill the auditorium in the presence of an audience.

It is important for the director and the production staff to understand that, during these run-through rehearsals, the vocal director must sit alone and be away from anyone in the auditorium who is talking aloud during the run-through (for example, the director giving notes to his assistant director or the lighting designer communicating cues to his assistant in the light booth). The vocal director at this stage needs to be totally focused upon the aural aspects of the production, and any person talking to or around the vocal director during the run-through can be very disruptive to his ability to take notes for the actors.

Frequently a director will discern certain vocal problems or potential vocal problems during the rehearsal process that he wants the vocal director to be listening for in the next run-through. It is extremely helpful if the director shares these concerns with the vocal director prior to the run-through of the play. By doing so, the vocal director is alerted in advance and is ready to make a detailed analysis for the director of the actors' voices at specific moments within the play.

Technical Rehearsals

During the sound/technical rehearsals, the vocal director should be present to serve as a consultant to the director, sound designer, and sound engineer in establishing an appropriate volume balance between the actors' voices and the production's recorded sound. The vocal director's primary concerns at this juncture of the rehearsal process are twofold: that the actors never need to strain their voices to be heard above the recorded sound and, secondly, that the recorded music and/or sound effects do not detract from the intelligibility of the actors' speaking voices.

If the actors are not needed full-time in the technical rehearsals for lighting and set changes, this time can be utilized for voice work. This period of the rehearsal process can prove an opportune time for the actors to consult with the vocal director regarding any problems or concerns they may still have concerning their vocal performance.

It is often advisable for the vocal director to take time off from the note-giving process on the night of the first dress rehearsal. Usually the actors are so absorbed with getting used to wearing and changing their costumes and makeup that any in-depth assessment of their vocal performance is not particularly helpful. In addition, the vocal director may find it helpful to get away from the production for a day so that he can come back refreshed and able to hear the production with greater objectivity.

Preview Performances

Preview performances prior to the official opening of a production provide the vocal director with valuable vocal assessment conditions. The auditorium is filled with audience members and the sounds of audience response are present to complete the acoustical and aural experience of the production. With an audience now present, fine-tuning can be done on all aspects of the actors' vocal life.

During the act breaks of preview performances, the vocal director may want to solicit audience feedback on the vocal life of the production with questions such as, "Are you able to hear the actors?," "Are there any characters whose lines you cannot understand?," "Is the story of the play clear to you?," "Are the dialects (if used) getting in the way of the intelligibility of the actors?" It is most informative to solicit feedback from a cross section of the audience, from senior citizens to young children. The feedback provided by these audience members is always instructive and invaluable, for they are listening to the play for the first time.

Opening Night and Beyond

If the vocal director, the actors, and the director have been in close communication throughout the final run-through stage, the voice notes tend to become fewer and fewer in number as opening night approaches. It is the goal of the vocal director to be able to honestly say to the actors after the last rehearsal, "Vocally, you are ready to open."

During the run of the show, vocal warm-ups prior to the play's performances should be led by a company member trained by the vocal director to assume this responsibility. It is extremely valuable for the actors if the vocal director can return to listen to the production on a weekly or biweekly basis to give feedback to the actors and address any concerns they may have regarding their voices now that they are actually experiencing the rigors of performance. It is not uncommon for actors in the professional theatre to give four or five performances of a play between Friday night and Sunday night. It is at vocally rigorous times such as these that actors can most appreciate the instruction, preparation, and guidance provided by the vocal director throughout the rehearsal process.

Chapter 5

The Vocal Director
and the Actor

It is the responsibility of the play's director to guide the actors in the interpretation of the language of the playscript. It is the vocal director's task to assist the director and the actors in achieving a clear and effective expression of this interpretation by means of the actors' voices and speech. Although every actor, character, and play present unique challenges for the vocal director, there are certain aspects of the vocal director's work that are common to every production.

The Vocal Warm-up and Its Function

The vocal warm-up serves several critical functions for the actor. It insures the actor's readiness to meet the heightened vocal demands of rehearsal and performance and encourages a disciplined approach to the work. The warm-up may be undertaken by the actor alone or with the other members of the acting company, but it should always involve a carefully ordered sequence of exercises aimed at achieving the following vocal demands:

1. Conscious relaxation
2. Physical flexibility and alignment
3. Awareness and strengthening of the breathing muscles—the "power mechanism" of the actor's voice
4. Vocal resonance
5. Pitch range flexibility
6. Voice strengthening
7. Articulatory flexibility and precision (including dialect drills as required)
8. Connecting the voice with inner impulses of thought and feeling
9. Vocal and physical transition into character

The Company Warm-up

While following the sequential order cited above, the company warm-up should be designed by the vocal director to address the specific needs of the acting company and the play they are about to perform. Throughout the rehearsal process patterns of voice/speech problems within the acting company will become evident. For example, the company may need more intensive work on articulatory clarity and pitch range flexibility than on voice strengthening. These areas of need can be emphasized by the vocal director in the company warm-up. Similarly, each play has its own specific voice/speech challenges. A play done in dialect, for example, will require dialect drills as a part of the company warm-up. Plays such as Sackler's *The Great White Hope* or Guare's *Six Degrees of Separation* require vocal warm-up exercises to insure that all moments of heightened vocal activity are produced by the actors without laryngeal/pharyngeal strain.

The company voice warm-up should be incorporated into the rehearsal and performance schedules. The timing of the warm-up is very important. In the rehearsal process, for example, the warm-up should come just before the actors begin their actual rehearsal, *not* before a note-giving session. If the acting company arrives at the theatre, goes through a vocal and physical warm-up, and then sits for half an hour while the stage director gives notes from the night before, all the energy generated by the warm-up will be diffused and dissipated. It is much more productive to have the actors receive their notes, warm-up, and then take the energy and concentration generated from the warm-up right into the rehearsal.

During the run of the show, the timing of the warm-up should be set according to the wishes of the cast, director, and stage manager. If there's an 8:00 P.M. curtain, for example, the company may choose to arrive at the theatre at 6:30 P.M. to do a twenty- to thirty-minute warm-up prior to getting into makeup and costume. Or the company may prefer to gather in costume and makeup at 7:15 P.M. to do a twenty-minute warm-up closer to curtain time. This latter scenario has the advantage of focusing the energies of the acting company moments before the actual performance, but the physicality of the exercises may have to be limited because of the actors' costumes and makeup. In addition, many actors require time for private preparation prior to performance and may find a group warm-up so close to curtain time to be disruptive. The nature of the show and the preferences of the actors should thus dictate the timing of the preshow warm-up.

The company warm-up is initially designed and taught by the vocal director. Except in those rare instances where a theatre has a vocal director on staff, the vocal director assigned to the production will need to prepare a company member to lead the warm-ups after the show opens. The vocal director's assistant should be a vocally trained individual respected by the company. The actor selected should not be a cast member with a major role, as this individual needs to be focusing on his vocal preparation, not that of the group. In executing this important function, the company warm-up leader should continue to approach the work in a highly professional manner, always adhere strictly to the time alloted, and be ever mindful of the purpose of the warm-up—to prepare the actors vocally for the heightened demands of stage performance.

Individual Warm-ups

Certain cast members may benefit from individually designed vocal warm-ups, especially if an actor has had no previous vocal training or if the role being created involves special voice/speech challenges, such as Lucky's articulatory tour de force in Beckett's *Waiting for Godot* or Puck's need to speak the play's language while engaged in heightened physical activity in Shakespeare's *A Midsummer Night's Dream*. In such instances, the vocal director can select specific exercises aimed at addressing the actor's special voice/speech needs both as self and as character. These individually designed warm-ups can be utilized by the actor in one-on-one sessions with the vocal director and as actor preparation prior to coming to rehearsal or performance.

Professional actors who have an extensive background in voice training often prefer to warm up on their own prior to rehearsal or performance. In such instances, the vocal director can serve as a resource to guide the focus of that actor's vocal preparation for a particular role and production.

The Note-taking Process

As discussed in the previous chapter, written notes serve as a valuable and efficient way for the vocal director to communicate with the actors throughout the rehearsal process. To insure that these notes are clearly and readily understood, the vocal director's note-taking symbols should be explained to the actors before rehearsals begin. The following symbols are very helpful in the note-taking process:

1. International Phonetic Alphabet symbols are invaluable for written notes regarding vowel and consonant pronunciation. Because IPA symbols cannot be communicated orally, however, the number system for vowel des-

ignation used by Arthur Lessac in his text *The Use and Training of the Human Voice* is invaluable for oral note giving.

2. ∧ and ∨ may be used to denote upward and downward inflection when specific words need highlighting, as in, "I wanted to go ∧ Saturday, not ∧ Sunday," or "He ∧ said he'd come to see me, ∨ but he never did".

3. Words that require stress are underlined, as in, "I said to go now!"

4. A circle around a word or phrase denotes that the actor needs to color that word or phrase to vividly convey an image or to let the audience hear clearly a character's thoughts or feelings toward what is being said, as in "The evening was (fabulous) !" or "I can't believe you'd consider marrying (Eddie Bostwick)."

5. A slash mark / denotes where the actor needs to take a breath.

6. Double slashes // indicate a shift in the character's objective. The audience needs to hear when a character moves from one objective to the next. New "units of action" must be aurally signaled by the actor's use of heightened vocal energy and appropriate vocal tone. For example, "You know, of course, that this is the last time we can be together like this. // Oh, it's no use. Where can I meet you tomorrow?"

Notes to the actors need to be written with clarity and intelligibility. If the vocal director has to explain orally what is meant by each written note or if his handwriting cannot be read by the actors, the whole timesaving aspect of giving written notes is defeated.

Vocal notes should be dated and the actors encouraged to save their written notes so that they can review them prior to the next day's rehearsal/performance. Frequently actors will say to the vocal director in regard to a vocal note, "Oh yes, I know what you mean, but at that particular moment I was struggling with my lines, tripping over my costume, focusing on my blocking, etc." to which the vocal director can respond, "Alright, but when that problem is solved, review and consider these observations regarding your vocal performance."

Lastly, it is helpful for the actors if each vocal note is proceeded by the page number in the text where the word or line occurs. For example: —p. 37 In the phrase, "I never could understand that man . . . " avoid nasality on the [æ] vowel in "understand", "that", and "man."

Getting Control of the Language

Since the play's language reveals the consciousness of the character, it is imperative that the actor get control of the language in the process of character development. This task involves the careful analysis of the words the playwright has chosen and the way the playwright has put those words together. Utilizing the director's interpretation of the play's language and characters to give focus to the work, the vocal director can help bring to the actors' attention numerous aspects of language analysis, including punctuation and pauses, breathing and phrasing, use of stress, inflection, coloration, and structural units and builds.

Punctuation and Pauses

In order to clearly and logically convey the meaning of the language, the actor must pay careful attention to punctuation in the script. It is through punctuation that the playwright provides the actor with directives regarding the grouping and phrasing of ideas and the place and length of pauses that separate those ideas. For example, a *period* denotes the completion of a thought. A *colon* signals a pause while, at the same time, it indicates the speaker's intention to continue on with an explanation, an example, a listing, an elaboration, or an extended quotation that is aimed at illuminating that which has preceded it. A *semi-colon* indicates "a degree of separation greater than that marked by the comma and less than that marked by the period. The semicolon is conventionally used to separate units that contain elements separated by commas, and to separate coordinate clauses having a relationship in meaning."[1] The *comma* is used to indicate a slight pause between sentence elements. The *dash* indicates a break in the sentence and the speaker's need to explain that which has gone before. The *question mark* forces the speaker to pause in anticipation of an answer. In instances where the speaker asking the question or questions does not pause, the question mark can take on the function of an exclamation mark. The *exclamation mark* denotes the completion of an expression or statement of strong emotion. *Ellipses* indicate that, although the speaker has stopped talking, the thought is being carried on. *Parentheses* surround words or phrases that qualify or explain that which has preceded. Parentheses not only signal a brief pause before the speaker utters the qualifying word or words, but most often the speaker employs downward or upward inflection to convey the parenthetical word or phrase. *Quotation marks* require that the actor pause before and after the word or words in quotations and give the quoted material special emphasis through the use of stress, intonation, coloration, and/or volume.

Breathing and Phrasing

The use of pauses not only serves to bring clarity to the meaning of spoken language, but provides the actor with ample opportunities to take refill breaths to support the voice. The actor's crucial task of discovering and executing the appropriate breathing and phrasing patterns for performance can be obtained in a two-step method. First, by analyzing the structure, punctuation, and meaning of the lines and then rehearsing the language aloud with the designated blocking *and* at performance volume with the theatre auditorium and the audience's presence in mind.

Vocal projection requires a sufficient and controlled breath supply, effective use of the resonating cavities to provide sound reinforcement for the initiated tone, and clear articulation. For ordinary everyday speech, the speaker does not require deep breathing. Speaking for the stage, however, requires a mode of voicing that is larger than life. Actors need to increase their breath support for greater volume, make optimum use of their resonating cavities, ennunciate actively, and always avoid laryngeal/pharyngeal strain. In moments of heightened vocal intensity on the stage, the actor may need to employ his full breath capacity to utter but a single word. Martha's extended "NOOOOOOooooooo" at the end of Albee's *Who's Afraid of Virginia Woolf?* is but one example. The amount of breath support required by the actor to vocally fill a theatre auditorium also depends upon the size and acoustics of a given theatre and the size of the audience.

Often actors rehearse in a small studio space, only to find that the breathing and phrasing patterns established during the rehearsal period no longer suffice when they move into a larger theatre for the final week of run-throughs. To enhance their volume in the larger space, they find themselves having to take deeper and more frequent breaths. The presence of an audience in the theatre and the resultant absorption of sound require the actors to project even more, and this can necessitate their making yet another adjustment in their breathing and phrasing patterns.

Actors in such a situation will frequently complain that they are suddenly being forced to perform at a volume level that goes against the sense of realism and truth that they experienced in the intimacy of the studio rehearsal space and that they are experiencing an unanticipated strain upon their vocal instruments. These continual adjustments in the actors' volume levels and breathing and phrasing patterns can be avoided if, with the guidance of the vocal director, the actors continuously rehearse with the theatre and audience in mind. By doing so, the actors can discover, early in the rehearsal process, a level of vocal expression that, not only feels truthful to them, but will also effectively serve the heightened vocal demands of performance.

Stressing Key Words

The actor gives clarity and meaning to the language of the play, not only through pauses and appropriate phrasing, but also through the use of stress. By emphasizing selected words, the actor conveys to the audience what is important within each phrase and sentence. Shakespeare's language, for example, can prove unintelligible to a modern audience if the actors do not clarify meaning through the use of stress. As Margaret Webster writes in her book *Shakespeare Without Tears:*

> It is always necessary to pick out the key words and to subordinate the less important ones which connect them. One director I know gives his actors the excellent advice: "Write out the speech as if it were a Western Union telegram. Then you won't have to pay for the inessentials."[2]

How does an actor know what to stress and what not to stress? Through the process of script analysis with the play's director and an increasing understanding of the character derived through working with the director in the rehearsal process, the actor begins to "think as character." By stressing those words that the *character* believes to be important, the actor reveals to the audience the character's inner thoughts and emotions.

Secondly, actors should be aware that stress is an important device for conveying exposition. They need to be alert to words that convey important background information necessary to making the story of the play clear to the audience; for example, when introducing names of people, places, times, events, etc.

Thirdly, words that are repeated by a character need to be stressed because their repetition reveals their importance to the character. Similarly, when a word is repeated in an exchange of dialogue between several characters that word requires stress, for it signals that the characters are listening and reacting to one another. For example,

CHARACTER A. "I'm going out with *Sarah.*"

CHARACTER B. "With *Sarah?*"

CHARACTER A. "Yes, *Sarah.*"

Inflection

Along with stress, inflection—a change in vocal pitch or tone—is the most expedient way for the speaker to convey to the listener what is important within a given phrase or sentence. For example, "I asked for a $\wedge$ cat, not a $\wedge$ dog." The highlighting of important words in a given phrase or sentence by means of inflection is necessary to convey exposition clearly and effectively, as well as parenthetical commentary, asides, antithetical thought, and passages of "verbal tennis." In speaking the play's language the actor is like the driver of a car navigating the twists and turns of an ever curving roadway, revealing through changes in pitch and tone the twists and turns of the character's consciousness.

In order to utilize inflection effectively, the actor needs to initiate vocalization within his optimal pitch range, approximately one fourth to one third above the actor's lowest comfortable speaking note. By doing so, the actor is free to make use of pitch variety through the use of upward and downward inflection in order to highlight key words and avoid the deadening effect of a monotone voice.

In the opening moments of Paul Zindel's *The Effect of Gamma Rays on Man-in-the-Moon Marigolds* the character Beatrice Hunsdorfer has an extensive monologue in the form of a telephone conversation and an exchange with her daughter Tillie that serves to convey important exposition about the play's characters and the circumstances of their lives. The actress playing Beatrice is charged with the task of making certain that the many important facts inherent in the language are conveyed to the audience at the start of the play. This can be accomplished in large part through the use of inflection. The decision to utilize upward or downward inflection on key words is the artistic choice of the actor. The sole criteria in this regard is to select the manner of inflection that best reveals the consciousness of the character at each particular moment in the play. Keeping in mind the important expository function of the following speech, the actress playing Beatrice might utilize inflection in the following manner:

> BEATRICE. (*To Tilly*) That ∧ school of yours is ∧ forty years behind the times anyway, and believe me you learn more around ∧ here than that ugly Mr. ∧ Goodman can teach you! You know, I really feel ∧ sorry for him. I never saw a man with a more ∧ effeminate face in my life. When I saw you talking to him by the ∧ lobster tank I said to myself, "Good lord, for a ∧ science teacher my poor girl's got herself a ∧ Hebrew ∧ hermaphrodite." Of course, he's not as bad as Miss ∧ Hanley. The idea of having her teach ∧ girl's ∧ gym is staggering. And ∧ you have to place ∧ me in the ∧ embarrassing position of giving them a reason to call me at ∧ eight-thirty in the morning, no less.[3]

Parenthetical commentary requires conscious awareness on the part of the actor in order to be voiced effectively. If an actor is speaking in too low a pitch overall, downward inflection for parenthetical commentary will be difficult if not impossible. Similarly, upward inflections will prove difficult to execute if the actor is speaking in too high a pitch. Once again, the decision to inflect up or down is the artistic choice of the actor. For example, "I like your dress, \/ but then I always did," or "Harry's really not that bad. \/ Not that I'd seriously consider dating him. /\ But, he's really not that bad." Parenthetical commentary can be great fun for the actor and an effective device for revealing the true consciousness of a character. By initiating his voice in an optimal pitch range, the actor will always "have somewhere to go" with pitch when explanations, qualifying information, or asides present themselves in the play's language. For example, note the use of parenthetical commentary in George's speech from Albee's *Who's Afraid of Virginia Woolf?*:

> GEORGE. . . . Martha, this young man is working on a system whereby chromosomes can be altered . . . well not all by himself— he probably has one or two co-conspirators—the genetic makeup of a sperm cell changed, reordered . . . *to* order, actually . . . for hair and eye color, stature, potency . . . I imagine . . . hairiness, features, health . . . and *mind* . . .[4]

Inflection also serves as a valuable tool for the actor in giving shape and meaning to lines of dialogue that embody antithesis. Antithesis refers to a contrast or opposition of thoughts, embodied in one or more phrases, clauses, or sentences. Hamlet's line "To be or not to be . . ." is a classic example of antithetical thought. In speaking antithetical dialogue it is the responsibility of the actor to set up one word or thought in opposition to another in order to clearly communicate the argument inherent in a given line or phrase. The use of inflection is an effective way of accomplishing this task. Instances of antithesis abound within the language of the theatre. Antithetical thought is highly theatrical, for it embodies conflict; the very substance of the drama. In Shakespeare's *As You Like It,* Phoebe's speech in Act III, scene v is filled with antitheses, and the actress taking the role of Phoebe must vocally play these antitheses if the audience is to clearly follow the character's vacillating feelings of disdain and longing.

> PHOEBE. Think not I love him, though I ask for him;
>   Tis but a peevish boy; yet he talks well.
>   But what care I for words? Yet words do well
>   When he that speaks them pleases those that hear.
>   It is a pretty youth; not very pretty;
>   But sure he's proud, and yet his pride becomes him . . .[5]

Inflection is also used by actors to negotiate through passages of "verbal tennis"—passages where a word or an idea is lobbed back and forth between characters, as in the following passage from Act II, scene i of Shakespeare's *The Taming of the Shrew*:

PETRUCHIO. Thy virtues spoke of, and thy beauty sounded,
　　　　　　Yet not so deeply as to thee belongs,
　　　　　　Myself am *mov'd* to woo thee for my wife.

KATHERINE. *Mov'd*! in good time. Let him that *mov'd*
　　　　　　you hither
　　　　　　Remove you hence. I knew you at the first
　　　　　　You were a *moveable*.

PETRUCHIO. Why, what's a *moveable*?

KATHERINE. A join'd *stool*.

PETRUCHIO. Thou has hit it; come, *sit* on me.

KATHERINE. *Asses* are made to *bear,* and so are *you*.

PETRUCHIO. *Women* are made to *bear,* and so are *you*.[6]

In speaking iambic pentameter verse in which the thought being expressed does not conclude within the ten syllable line, but carries over to the following line or lines, the actor must shape the verse by giving a slight upward inflection to the last word of the line before continuing on to the next verse line. This will enable the listener to absorb what has been said before the actor continues on to finish the thought. Note how in Shakespeare's *Richard III*, Act I, scene i, Richard III's first complete thought encompasses four lines of verse, with a brief pause denoted by a semi-colon after the second line.

RICHARD III. Now is the winter of our /\ discontent
　　　　　　Made glorious summer by this sun of York;
　　　　　　And all the clouds that lour'd upon our /\ house
　　　　　　In the deep bosom of the ocean buried.[7]

The slight poise and upward inflection needed to define the shape of a verse line which is not end-stopped by punctuation is also needed at a caesura, which is a break or grammatical pause within a line of verse. In her book *The Actor and His Text,* Cicely Berry writes:

> Because of the length of a five-beat line, there is nearly always a break within the line, in most cases after the second or third stressed syllable. Sometimes this break coincides with a full-stop or a colon, and so with a break in thought. But more often . . . it is simply a poise on a word— i.e., the word holds and lifts for a fraction of a moment before it plunges into the second half of the line. This poise is necessary for the ear of the listener in that it allows a space, a still moment, for us to check the key word in the line—to throw it up as it were. Now the quicker we are speaking, the more the shape needs to be observed. Very often, when we do not understand a speech, it is because this shaping has not been attended to.[8]

Hermia's speech in Act III, ii of *A Midsummer Night's Dream* provides an excellent example of what we are talking about. By employing a brief poise on the words preceding the caesuras, the actor gives shape and clarity to the rapidly spoken verse.

> HERMIA. Now I perceive that she hath made compare
>   Between our *statures*; she hath urged her height,
>   And with her *personage,* her tall personage,
>   Her height, for *sooth,* she hath prevailed with him.
>   And are you grown so high in his esteem,
>   Because I am so dwarfish and so low?
>   How low am *I?* thou painted maypole? Speak!
>   How low am *I?* I am not yet so low
>   But that my nails can reach unto thine eyes.[9]

Coloration

It has long been said that "the eyes are the window to the soul." One can also say that the voice is the true conveyor of an individual's personality, thought, and feeling. In his book *Keep Your Voice Healthy,* Dr. Friedrich Brodnitz states, "It is not a powerful instrument, this human voice, nor a technically perfect one. A trumpet can blow louder, a violin can play faster, an oboe can spin longer melodies. Still, it is unsurpassed in expressivity, depth and soulfulness of tone, truly the queen of the instruments."[10]

By coloring the language of the character through the use of tone variance and word play, the actor reveals to the audience the character's inner feelings and attitudes towards his world and the other characters who inhabit that world. To color the play's language effectively, the actor must fully understand the character's attitudes towards all aspects of his life; that is, the actor must be fully immersed in the process of "thinking as character." Imagine how differently the word "husband" would sound from the lips of Juliet in *Romeo and Juliet* as opposed to that of Hedda in *Hedda Gabler*. Or consider how the word "honor" would be spoken by John Proctor in *The Crucible* as opposed to Valmont in *Les Liaisons Dangereuses*. Through the process of "thinking as character," the actor allows the words and their inherent images and connotations to be filtered through the character's persona. And, because acting is reacting, the actor must possess the capacity to listen to his fellow actors with an acute awareness and sensitivity, allowing their expressions of thought and feeling to influence and inform a vocal response.

Giving coloration and expressiveness to the play's language represents a vocal challenge for the actor that often requires extensive training, for in real life most individuals practice vocal control rather than vocal expressiveness. Heightened emotionality has the potential to upset others by forcing them out of their own comfortable rhythms and sense of control. Displays of emotion can be threatening, annoying, and disruptive. In today's society, a high value is placed upon emotional control and, as societal beings, we coexist through mutually accepted modes of behavior. But, as has been stated before, the theatre is not real life. Drama presents conflict, not equanimity. Plays are about people who are struggling to attain something, not about individuals who "have it all together." The theatre requires the actor to have freedom of emotional expression. This being the case, the actor must undergo an extensive period of retraining. The actor's capacity for vocal expressiveness must be developed through exercises designed to bring the actor's vocal life into more direct contact with his own psychological, intellectual, and emotional impulses, as well as with those of the character being created.

Structure

The problem of "generalizing"—speaking the words of the play in a general mood or attitude—is one of the most common traps for the actor. By generalizing an extended monologue, for example, the actor conveys an emotion or attitude to the audience, but not the sense of the lines. The audience is left saying to themselves, "I know the character is angry, happy, proud, etc., but I have no idea *what* he was saying." To avoid this problem, it is imperative that the actor break down the language of an extended monologue or scene into beats—small units of action that encompass the beginning to the end of a single intention. In performance, the actor needs to begin each new beat with a renewed vocal energy and a vocal tone appropriately reflective of the character's shift in thought or feeling. In doing so, the actor will avoid making the monologue or scene sound the same from beginning to end and will allow the audience to follow the twists and turns of the character's consciousness. Note the many beat shifts (designated below by an // marking) inherent in Faulkland's extended monologue from Act III, scene iii of Richard Brinsley Sheridan's *The Rivals*:

> FAULKLAND. In tears! stay Julia, stay but for a moment. // The door is fastened! // Julia!—my soul—but for one moment— // I hear her sobbing! // 'Sdeath! what a brute am I to use her thus! // Yet stay—aye—she is coming now: // how little resolution there is in woman!—how a few soft words can turn them! // No, faith!— she is *not* coming either. // Why, Julia—my love—say but that you forgive me—come but to tell me that— // now, this is being *too* resentful: // stay! she *is* coming too— // I thought she would— no steadiness in anything! Her going away must have been a mere trick then— // she shan't see that I was hurt by it. I'll affect indifference—(*Hums a tune: then listens*) // —no—zounds! she's *not* coming!—nor don't intend it, I suppose. This is not steadiness, but obstinacy! // Yet I deserve it. What, after so long an absence, to quarrel with her tenderness! // —'twas barbarous and unmanly! I should be ashamed to see her now. // I'll wait till her just re-sentment is abated— // and when I distress her so again, may I lose her for ever! and be linked instead to some antique virago, whose gnawing passions, and long-hoarded spleen, shall make me curse my folly half the day and all the night! (*Exit*)[11]

By providing distinct vocal variations for the beats designated above, the actor playing Faulkland will avoid playing the speech as the generalized ramblings of an hysterical lover. By voicing the monologue with the thought and vocal transitions in mind, the actor will be better able to navigate through the monologue, revealing the wealth of character information inherent in the language: Faulkland's overwrought nature, his turbulent relationship with Julia, his self-recriminations for his mistreatment of her, and his ambivalent feelings toward Julia in particular and women in general.

Vocal "Builds"

Just as every play has a structure, so does each act, scene, and extended monologue within the play. The actor's use of vocal "builds" helps define this inherent structure for the audience. By carefully analyzing the structural "builds" within each line, extended monologue, scene, and act, the actor and the director avoid the monotony that can occur when a play is performed from start to finish at the same level of intensity. Perhaps the most common use for "builds" is to convey to the audience that a structural unit of the play is reaching its culmination. For example, "builds" are written into the language of the play as a means by which the playwright signals a character's exit; the end of a beat within a continuing scene; or the end of a monologue, scene, or act. In Herb Gardner's *A Thousand Clowns,* for example, note how the playwright uses music and the voices of Murray, Nick, and Sandra to aurally build to the end of the play.

> MURRAY. (*He continues to talk out the window, softly at first.*) Well, then if you're not ready, we better work on the Military March number. Now the last time we ran this, let's admit it was pretty ragged. I mean, the whole "Spirit of '76" float was in disgraceful shape yesterday—O.K. now, let's go, everybody ready—(*Nick looks up from his work at the carton, smiles at what Murray is saying out the window. Nick picks up record from bed, puts it on record-player, turns PLAYER on.*) Grenadiers ready, Cavalry ready, Cossacks ready, Rough Riders ready, Minute Men ready—(*The RECORD PLAYER has warmed up now and we hear "Stars and Stripes Forever." Murray hears the music, turns from the window, smiling, acknowledges Nick's assistance; turns to the window again, his voice gradually growing in volume.*) O.K. now, let's go—ready on the cannons, ready on the floats, ready on the banners, ready on the flags—(*The MUSIC builds up with Murray's voice, Nick humming along with the band and Sandra laughing as Murray shouts.*) Let's go—let's go—(*THE CURTAIN FALLS*).

Vocal Highlighting

Vocal highlighting refers to the increased vocal energy required of the actor at various key moments throughout the play. Whenever appropriate, the actor should vocally "take the stage" at the start of new acts and scenes, arresting the focus of the audience by means of increased volume and vocal energy. Secondly, heightened vocal energy is required by the actor when making an entrance. Any entrance of a character signals a new unit of action within the play's structure and requires vocal highlighting. Thirdly, each scene of a play needs to be analyzed in terms of its individual beats or units of intention, so that the actors can begin each new scene beat with a renewed vocal energy and tonal quality appropriate to that beat. In doing so, actors will avoid generalizing; that is, giving a scene the same sound and intensity from beginning to end. And, fourthly, the actor who utters the final line of each scene and act should, whenever it is appropriate, infuse that line with added vocal energy and a tone of finality. We in the audience should *hear* that a scene is over. When a scene just "trails off," it loses its impact as a distinct structural unit of the whole. When the audience does not *hear* that an act has ended, they will often demonstrate their confusion by withholding applause until a visual cue—such as lights coming up in the auditorium— tells them that the act is over. Actors and directors need to be alert to this common occurrence in the theatre. All too often actors will depart from the stage at the end of an act, the lights will come down on the stage and come up in the auditorium, and the confused audience members will turn to each other and ask, "Is this the intermission?" Meanwhile, the impact of the act has been dissipated. This problem can be remedied by having the actors vocally highlight the beginnings and endings of the play's scenes and acts, thereby insuring that the play's structure is given aural definition.

Avoiding the Whispering Mode

In moments of intense emotion on the stage, actors often pull their voices back into a whispering mode. This is done for a number of reasons. The actor may fear "taking the lid off" his own emotions and will attempt to control the character's emotions by pulling them inward and whispering the lines. Also, whispering may make the actor feel more intense, and he will therefore assume he is having a like effect upon the audience. The reality is that whispering has little visceral impact upon the listener, be it the actor's scene partner or the audience. The human voice, like any musical instrument, attracts the listener by virtue of its tonal resonance. It is through the *sound* of the voice that emotions are shared with the listener. An actor who employs a whispering mode in the expression of his character's thoughts and feelings will find it difficult to maintain the audience's interest. In addition, persistent use of a "stage whisper" can strain the vocal folds. The key to having actors perform without strain and vocal injury is to make sure that the actor's voice is well-placed *at all times* and especially during moments of high emotionality on the stage. The vocal director, in collaboration with the stage director, needs to make the actors aware of these facts and their tendency to employ the whispering mode through constant coaching: "Don't sit on the emotion. Let it out through your voice."

Pronunciation and Articulation

The actor's speech presents two major concerns for the vocal director: pronunciation and articulation. Pronunciation involves the utterance of specific phonemes, the placement of stress, and the use of appropriate inflection. The character's mode of pronunciation reveals to the audience many aspects of his identity, such as his regional or ethnic origins, educational level, self-image, and social and cultural affiliations. The actor's mode of pronunciation is thus a major factor in the process of character revelation. In the theatre no mode of pronunciation or dialect is superior to another. Rather, it is the actor's challenge to utilize that mode of pronunciation which is most *appropriate* for the character. For example, the character of Beatrice in Paul Zindel's *The Effect of Gamma Rays on Man-in-the-Moon Marigolds* is an emotionally disturbed woman who disliked formal education and struggled to get through high school. Because of her own ignorance, self-pity, and alcoholism she unwittingly inflicts a great deal of psychological violence upon her two teenage daughters during the course of the play. Several years ago I attended a production of the play in which the actress playing Beatrice spoke her lines with flawless Standard American pronunciation, making the character sound like a highly cultured, aware, and educated college graduate. As a result, the character's relationships and actions within the play took on a sinister and sadistic quality; far from what Zindel had written or intended.

Whether the language of the play is formal and elevated or informal and colloquial and whether the actors are speaking in Standard American or a regional dialect, active articulation is always required to meet the theatrical need of intelligibility. Actors often wrongly presume that because a play is written in colloquial language they can "get by" with a mumbling mode of speech. They need to be reminded that it is the character's vocabulary and mode of pronunciation that conveys informality to the audience. Mumbled, incoherent words convey nothing.

In performing classic plays nothing proves more helpful to the actor in achieving an elevated acting style than the use of precise and active articulation. Mumbling, slurred or omitted consonants, substituting one consonant for another are the hallmarks of contemporary, informal speech. Fullness and precision of diction lend stature and authority to a character and give that character an aural "presence" on the stage.

Sometimes an actor will use a mumbling mode of speech, not because he is incapable of articulating more fully, but because the actor is feeling insecure regarding some aspect of the role. Just as an actor will use a whispering mode to control moments of intense emotional expression, many actors mumble to hide their uncertainties regarding how to voice a given line as character. When an actor consistently mumbles certain lines of dialogue, it may be due to the fact that the actor is unable to commit fully to the vocal expression of the character's thoughts and feelings at that particular moment in the play. This is an acting problem, not a vocal problem, and needs to be addressed by the play's director in consultation with the actor.

Obscure, Archaic, and Difficult Words

A director colleague once said, "The greatest sin a theatre artist can commit is to make the audience say, 'Whaaa'?" When the language of the play embodies obscure or archaic words and phrases, the actor must help the audience by paying special attention to how these words are spoken. Difficult words can be clearly conveyed if the actor speaks them with precise articulation, highlights them by use of stress and/or inflection, and colors the words to make them sound like what they mean. It is also helpful to set the word off with a brief pause before and after its utterance. When necessary, an appropriate physical gesture can also be helpful in illuminating for the audience the meaning of the word. The actress playing Viola in Shakespeare's *Twelfth Night*, for example, must take all these suggestions into account when speaking the difficult word "fadge" in her line in Act II, scene iii "How will this *fadge?*" (meaning "How will this all succeed or work out?") The same holds true for the actress playing Lady Anne in Shakespeare's *Richard III* Act I, scene ii when, in response to Richard's line "Thine eyes, sweet lady, have infected mine," Lady Anne retorts: "Would they were *basilisks*, to strike thee dead!" (the word "basilisk" referring to a mythical lizardlike monster with supposedly fatal breath and glance).

Moving and Speaking

During the rehearsal process, the vocal director needs to alert the actors to those moments in the play when physical action is hindering the intelligibility of the lines. For example, when an actor is speaking lines while crossing upstage or yelling invectives while lunging toward another actor in a moment of physical violence; or, when two actors are speaking to one another while engaged in a sword fight or highly physical love scene. Physical movement, especially movement that is inherently dramatic, has the potential to detract from the spoken word. The actor needs to be aware of this fact and take special care with the language at such moments in the play.

Dialects

In *Stage Dialects* Jerry Blunt writes:

> A stage dialect is a normal dialect altered as needed to fit the requirements of theatrical clarity and dramatic interpretation. . . . The alteration may be slight or marked, may be merely suggested or strongly distorted, may make sounds more melodious or more harsh, dramatic or comedic. Consequently, a stage dialect has the double duty of achieving factual truthfulness through fidelity to its primary sources and artistic truthfulness through fidelity to dramatic interpretation.[13]

The use of dialects in the theatre adds color and richness to the aural texture of a production. A dialect informs the audience of many aspects of a character's identity: place of birth and/or residence, ethnic and cultural background, level of education, and social class. A stage dialect informs the audience about each individual character as does a stage costume. Each dialect must be fashioned to meet the specific needs of a given character, for each character possesses an individual variation of the dialect. An Irishman who has lived in America for many years and has been educated at Harvard, for example, will speak differently than an Irishman who has never left his native homeland.

It is the responsibility of the vocal director to instruct each actor regarding the dialect's resonance placement, phoneme substitutions, lilt or intonation, and rhythm, and to bring to the actor's attention the idiom, word order, and grammatical changes provided by the playwright. Throughout the rehearsal process the vocal director listens for dialect consistency and intelligibility, and the optimal balance between authenticity and theatrical clarity. A stage dialect should serve to reveal the character to the audience. If a dialect is too strong, it can "upstage" the character and obscure the meaning of the language. This must not be allowed to happen. In such cases the vocal director must guide the actor in modifying the dialect to its most effective level of intelligibility.

If the actors are familiar with the vocal director's notation system and have learned the IPA in the process of dialect acquisition, then the vocal director's note-taking process is greatly expedited. Dialect notes can be rapidly recorded by underlining the mispronounced phoneme in a given word and supplying the phonetic symbol for the required sound. For example, a written critique of an American actor employing a British dialect might be notated as follows:

Ought [ɔ:], not [ɔ]
Tone [əou], not [ou]
Secretary [rI], not [Eri]

Minor Characters

Less experienced directors often neglect the preparation of actors who speak only one line or several lines within a production. This lack of attention to detail can have quite a negative impact on a play in performance. The characters of the Sheriff in Eugene O'Neill's *Desire Under the Elms*, Fortinbras in Shakespeare's *Hamlet*, or the two policemen (Lieb and Moran) in O'Neill's *The Iceman Cometh* have relatively few lines, but in each case the characters' lines come at the very end of their respective dramas where the maintenance of mood and intensity is crucial. There are, of course, no unimportant lines or unimportant characters in a playscript. The playwright has written every character and line to contribute to the play's overall impact, and the vocal life of each of the play's characters must be carefully attended to by the director as well as the vocal director.

Actors who speak but one or two lines in a play often voice their lines with less energy than those actors who are playing major roles. This usually happens when the actor is a less experienced performer or is under-rehearsed by the director. The vocal director must be alert to this common occurrence and make sure that the overall vocal energy of a scene is not diminished by an actor's hesitancy or lack of technical preparation. The actor must be instructed to "take the scene vocally" on his line(s) and be made to understand that, if the words he speaks were not important to the play, the playwright would not have written them.

Balancing Human and Nonhuman Sounds

It is the vocal director's responsibility, in consultation with the director and the sound designer, to insure that there is a proper balance between the play's human and nonhuman sounds so that the two are never in conflict with each other. Peter Weiss' *Marat Sade* and Eugene O'Neill's *The Hairy Ape* are but two examples of plays that require careful, detailed orchestration of the human and nonhuman sounds. Several years ago I attended a production of *The Hairy Ape* in which the director took O'Neill's Act I, scene i stage direction—*"The curtain rises on a tumult of sound"*—to an extreme. Throughout much of the play's first scene, the roar of the ship's engine and the banging of the stokers' shovels drowned out the voices of the actors. Key exposition was lost, and the audience was unable to understand the story of the play. The theatre would have been more accurate had they advertised "An Evening of Visceral Sound Effects" rather then Eugene O'Neill's *The Hairy Ape*, for audience members were denied the opportunity to hear much of the play's language.

Hidden Objectives

Often actors become vocally trapped by "hidden objectives," that is speaking the lines with some personal objective in mind rather than that of the character. For example, an actor might be thinking, "I'm afraid of or uncertain about this particular moment in the play, so I'm going to control the utterance of my lines here" (for example, by whispering or mumbling the lines or delivering them with a tight-jawed mode of enunciation). Or, "At this point in the play I'm going to show the audience what wonderful resonance, vocal power, or diction I have." Such "hidden objectives" get in the way of an actor's full and truthful revelation of character. An experienced and sensitive vocal director should learn to discern when "hidden objectives" are causing vocal problems and, in consultation with the director and the actor, make the actor aware of the effect these "hidden objectives" are having upon his character's vocal image. Except in those special instances when a character is *trying* to employ a "character voice" for one reason or another (for example, Bottom trying to imitate a great tragedian in the "play within the play" in *A Midsummer Night's Dream* or Lord Fancourt Babberly impersonating Donna Lucia D'Alvadorez in *Charley's Aunt*), it should never be the actor's intention to create a "character voice." Rather it is the challenge of the actor to "think as character" and, in the process, allow his voice to reflect truthfully his character's inner consciousness.

Working with the "Wonderful Voice"

On occasion, vocal directors have the opportunity and challenge of working with actors who have deep, booming, resonant voices. The joy of working

with such actors is that they usually possess very healthy vocal instruments
and the sound of their voices gives them a high degree of charisma on the
stage. The challenge lies in the fact that the highly resonant tone of such a
voice can, *if* other vocal skills are absent, "upstage" the meaning of the lines
by placing the audience's attention solely on the tonal quality of the voice.
A theatre audience can become lulled by a beautiful voice and miss the
meaning of the lines and/or focus upon the actor as actor rather than the
actor as character.

It is not uncommon for an actor who has the potential for highly resonant
vocalization to repress the full and effective usage of his instrument on the
stage due to the fact that, for many years, people in his offstage life have
said, "Quiet down. You are talking too loud!" In an attempt to control his
volume in everyday life, the actor may have resorted to using minimal oral
space while speaking (i.e. mumbling) and may have confined his voice to his
lower pitch range in an attempt to control volume; the latter resulting in a
monotone mode of speaking. In working with actors who exhibit these tend-
encies, I have found it helpful to incorporate the following exercise into their
daily vocal warm-up:

Exercise.   Hold your finger or a pencil approximately four inches from your
mouth as if it were a radio microphone and explore your lines at a low volume
level with emphasis upon active lip activity, utilization of your optimal pitch
range, fullness of articulation, appropriate use of stress and inflection, and
coloration. By taking away volume and the "booming" vocal tone while
maintaining forward placement of the voice, the actor is forced to explore
the other designated aspects of effective speaking that may not have been
exercised and developed heretofore.

The actor with the "wonderful voice" may have received abundant praise
for his voice all of his adult life and, therefore, may never have perceived the
need for vocal education and training. The actor may be ignorant of the
principles of vocal production, vocal health care, and the special vocal demands of acting for the stage. He may, therefore, be more likely to engage
in vocally abusive behavior in rehearsal and performance than the less en-
dowed actor who has had an extensive education in vocal health and production. A "wonderful voice" may deteriorate noticeably within several years
time if the actor continues to perform without a sound knowledge of his
vocal instrument and how to care for it.

Notes

1. *Webster's New World Dictionary of the American Language* (New York: The World Publishing Company, 1960), p. 1324.

2. Margaret Webster, *Shakespeare Without Tears* (Greenwich, Connecticut: Fawcett Publications, Inc., 1964), p. 67.

3. Paul Zindel, *The Effect of Gamma Rays on Man-in-the-Moon Marigolds* (New York: Dramatists Play Service, Inc., 1970), p. 9.

4. Edward Albee, *Who's Afraid of Virginia Woolf?* (New York: Dramatists Play Service, Inc., 1962), p. 33.

5. William Shakespeare, *As You Like It* in *The Complete Plays and Poems of William Shakespeare*. Edited by William Allan Neilson and Charles Jarvis Hill (Cambridge, Massachusetts: The Riverside Press, 1942), p. 233.

6. William Shakespeare, *The Taming of the Shrew* in *The Complete Plays and Poems of William Shakespeare*. Edited by William Allan Neilson and Charles Jarvis Hill (Cambridge, Massachusetts: The Riverside Press, 1942), pp. 159–60.

7. William Shakespeare, *Richard III* in *The Complete Plays and Poems of William Shakespeare*. Edited by William Allan Neilson and Charles Jarvis Hill (Cambridge, Massachusetts: The Riverside Press, 1942), p. 859.

8. Cicely Berry, *The Actor and His Text* (New York: Charles Scribner's Sons, 1987), p. 58.

9. William Shakespeare, *A Midsummer Night's Dream*. Edited by Wolfgang Clemen (New York: The New American Library, Inc., 1963), p. 89.

10. Dr. Friedrich Brodnitz, *Keep Your Voice Healthy* (Boston: College Hill Press, 1988), p. 21.

11. Richard Brinsley Sheridan, *The Rivals*. Edited by Elizabeth Duthie (London: A & C Black, 1990), pp. 60–61.

12. Herb Gardner, *A Thousand Clowns* (New York: Samuel French, Inc., 1962), pp. 93–94.

13. Jerry Blunt, *Stage Dialects* (San Francisco: Chandler Publishing Co., 1967), p. 1.

Chapter 6

The Special Vocal Demands of the Stage Actor

Good physical and vocal health are top priorities for the actor. Indeed, good health supercedes everything; if an actor is physically or vocally indisposed and cannot perform, it matters very little how talented that actor may be. The greatest threats to the vocal health of the actor are lack of training and knowledge of the vocal mechanism, vocal misuse and abuse, stress, and undisciplined behaviors.

Training

The vocal and physical training of an actor has much in common with the training of a professional athlete. Actors must build strength and stamina, cultivate behaviors that help insure good health, learn to make optimum use of their physical instruments, acquire the ability to perform under conditions of stress and public observation, and learn to concentrate all their physical and mental powers toward the attainment of a specific objective.

But the vocal and physical training of the actor differs from that of the athlete in a significant way: the actor's voice and body must be attuned and made directly responsive to the thoughts and emotions of the various characters he portrays. The actor is the vehicle through which a character, as written by the playwright, is vocally and physically conveyed to the audience. It matters little in the theatre if an actor fully experiences a character's consciousness in performance if the audience is not made to share in the experience. As a famous Broadway actor once said, "It doesn't matter a damn what I feel on the stage if the lady in the second row who paid $50.00 for her seat doesn't feel it!"

The actor's work is twofold: the actor's work on himself and the actor's work on his role. Voice care and training are an integral part of the actor's art and involve the following:

1. Ongoing training of the vocal instrument to gain control over the basics of efficient, effective, and healthful vocal production;

2. The development of the voice as an instrument of expression capable of conveying to an audience the character's inner thoughts and feelings as well as the exact nature of the character's attitudes and relationships toward himself, others, and the world around him;
3. The development of the actor as a highly attuned and sensitive listener so that he remains ever aware of the enormous potential of the voice for human expression and character revelation;
4. The development of the actor's capacity to integrate selected voice and speech attributes as part of the process of character creation. In regard to the pronunciation aspects of character creation, the actor needs to have a thorough knowledge of phonetics and a systematic approach to learning dialects.

The sound of a character's voice and the way the character speaks is a direct result of that character's unique background and mode of behavior. The actor needs to consider these facts in terms of every role he creates. Just as we never meet two persons in life who are exactly alike, so you will never find two identical characters in dramatic literature. That which constitutes the difference between them is what makes each character unique. Every character presents a multitude of challenges for the actor, not the least of which is the character's vocal life. Clearly, the actor who fails to train his voice for the demands of the profession will not only be lacking in range of artistic creativity, but, like the poorly conditioned athlete, will be placing himself in serious risk of vocal injury.

Misuse and Abuse

The process of character creation and the act of performing that character upon the stage are complex and demanding endeavors in which the actor's vocal instrument is taxed to a much greater degree than in normal everyday usage. If actors are called upon to utilize their voices in ways that they are unaccustomed to doing and not trained to do, then they run the risk of injury. Any professional athlete or dancer knows the importance of physical preparation. Professionals condition their bodies daily in order to keep them at peak performance level. If long periods of time pass without disciplined exercise, then the potential for injury in performance is heightened.

Theatre is larger than life. Therefore, the actor's mode of vocal expression must be larger than life. Whatever the character is thinking and feeling must be vocally conveyed by the actor through the use of appropriate volume and levels of expression whether the actor is performing in a small studio theatre or a large, three-balcony auditorium.

The actor is also required to sustain heightened vocal energy for extended periods of time. Rehearsals are often long and exhausting, and the task of character creation is a strenuous one—mentally, physically, and emotionally. Professional actors usually perform seven or eight times per week. Depending upon the play and the role, this performance schedule can place great demands upon the actor's voice. Vocal stamina—the ability to resist vocal fatigue and injury—is thus an essential attribute for the actor.

Professional actors are protected from inordinately long rehearsals by the rules of the Actors' Equity Association that places limits upon the amount of time an actor can rehearse in a given day. But nonunion actors rehearse according to the dictates of the director. All too often, in non-equity theatre, directors work with a "we'll stay until we get it right" mentality. Ignorant or unmindful of the actors' vocal training and capabilities and indifferent to the fact that the actors may have put in an eight-hour work day prior to rehearsal, a zealous and uninformed director can place his actors in a situation where vocal overuse, misuse, and abuse are likely to occur.

In order to insure the health and optimal functioning of his speaking voice, the actor needs to have a thorough understanding of how his voice is produced, knowledge of how to maintain vocal health, extensive and ongoing training, a dedication to daily vocal exercise prior to a rehearsal or performance, and a disciplined awareness of optimum voice usage at *all* times. In addition, the actor needs to be able to analyze the special vocal demands of a given role. He must then have the willingness and patience to approach these demands on a highly conscious and technical level within the rehearsal process until, through repetition, their healthful and effective execution becomes integral to the character's mode of expression. I call this "vocal choreography." Most actors readily accept the necessity of choreographing moments of physical violence on the stage in order to prevent physical injury, but they often fail to understand the necessity of "vocal choreography" to insure the healthful execution of moments of high emotional intensity. Indeed, the greater the actor's emotional expression on the stage, the more conscious the actor must be in regard to vocal execution. If this is not the case, the actor may deliver a vocally impassioned opening night performance, but will, most likely, find himself with a hoarse voice and reduced vocal endurance in subsequent performances, *if* he can sustain the run at all.

In the process of character creation, the actor utilizes his voice, body, mind, and emotions to create another human being as seen by the playwright for the stage. During rehearsals, the actor will often experience the emotions of the character. He must then find a way to convey these emotions effectively, theatrically, and healthfully night after night to an audience. Plays are about people in conflict whose lives are frequently filled with emotional intensity.

Playwrights write about people who are struggling and fighting for something; people in trouble. The actor must be solid enough in the control of his own technique to insure that the tension of the character does not become his own personal tension. For example, when Shakespeare's Richard III desperately cries out, "A horse! a horse! my kingdom for a horse!" (V, iv), he is crying out for a means to save his life. In the early stages of the rehearsal process, the actor must approach the utterance of these lines with a split mental focus. As character, the actor is thinking, "I must get a horse to ride or I shall die!" As craftsman, the actor must simultaneously be saying to himself, "Keep your throat relaxed. Call the words in your middle pitch range. Use vowel extension. Take a breath before 'A horse!' Take another breath before the next 'a horse!' Take another breath before 'My kingdom for a horse!' " This mental "juggling" act can be made less awkward if the actor pinpoints such moments of technical difficulty early in the rehearsal period and, through the process of repetition, makes the means of execution an integral part of the character's behavior. The actor allows the character's thoughts, feelings, manner of movement and voicing to be "housed" in his mind, heart, and body. But in performing the role, a part of the actor's consciousness must always be monitoring the execution of his character's physical and vocal expression so that he does not inflict injury upon himself or others.

An actor must be capable of employing variables of voice and speech appropriate to the character being created. These variables may include modifications in the actor's own voice in terms of pitch, volume, rate, rhythm, enunciation, pronunciation, and intensity. With a full knowledge and control over his vocal mechanism, the actor can experiment with various modes of voice and speech and, through repetition within the rehearsal process, make them intrinsic to the character as well as theatrically effective. Vocally untrained actors, however, risk harm to their vocal mechanisms in trying to effect a mode of voicing that is not their own. They do not understand that, in adopting an unnatural voice, they may be putting a great deal of strain upon their vocal folds; more specifically, the vocal fold mucosa or surface layer of the vocal folds. This strain, combined with the necessity to sustain the unnatural mode of voicing for long periods of time and at a louder than normal volume, can result in vocal injury. The classic example of this is the young, untrained actor who tenses his throat muscles and adopts a throaty sound to impersonate an old person or a tough gangster. Optimal vocal production occurs when the throat is open and relaxed so that it can serve as an efficient resonating cavity. Use of throat tension is, therefore, not a healthy option for character creation. Inevitably, young actors will say, "Then how can I sound old?" or "How can I sound tough?" Speaking in a throaty voice is but one way to convey age and toughness and a stereotypic one at that. It is preferable for actors playing age or "tough guys" to experiment with minor changes in their use of rate, intensity, stress, pitch variety, pronunciation, and word coloration to reveal the inner consciousness of the character. The bottom line is that, if the actor's voice as character is not efficiently produced, the new and imposed vocal mode can undermine the effectiveness of the actor's performance and potentially do harm to his vocal mechanism.

Without knowledge of their vocal mechanisms, sufficient training, daily care and conditioning, and a conscious, craftsmanlike working out of special vocal demands within the rehearsal process, actors will always be prone to vocal abuse and injury in rehearsal and performance. Incidents of vocal abuse, often occurring in moments of heightened emotional expression, are not uncommon to vocally untrained actors. All too often a director who has worked conceptually on a production for many months will find his work undermined in the last days of the rehearsal process by an actor who has injured his voice. Though the director and the other actors in the production may be sympathetic, the reality is that the vocally impaired actor has, through lack of training and incorrect voice usage, jeopardized the success of the production. Highly trained and educated actors and directors working in collaboration with a vocal director can minimize such needless incidents of acute vocal injury.

Illness vs. Injury

In maintaining optimal vocal health, it is important for the actor to understand the distinction between voice problems that are the direct result of illness and those caused by functional misuse and abuse of the vocal mechanism. Noted otolaryngologist Dr. Robert Bastian, who has had extensive experience in treating actors and singers, addresses this distinction between vocal injury and illness as follows:

> Every performer is going to have instances of illness—a severe cold with laryngitis or flu, for example—when they simply cannot perform. Becoming ill is something that happens to us all. But some actors and singers tend to consider every instance of vocal indisposition as being related to illness whereas, in my experience, incidents of illness cause far less chronic vocal indisposition than does self-inflicted (though not intentionally self-inflicted) functional vocal abuse. The fact is that, no matter how good the actor or singer is, he is still participating in a profession which involves "high risk" vocal behavior. By far the great majority of chronic voice

problems which take more than three weeks to overcome result from the individual's vocal behavior.

It is important for the performer to understand the difference between illness and injury because, if the performer incorrectly thinks that his voice problems are the result of illness, he will go from doctor to doctor looking for "a pill" to cure his "illness" while ignoring the fact that his vocal problems are most likely the result of personal, vocal, and general behavior. In a sense, an illness is the doctor's responsibility. Whereas an injury involves the actor taking most of the responsibility for recovery. Patients with vocal injury often feel guilty. I reassure them that nobody intends to injure themselves vocally, but unless they recognize the true origin of the problem, they can't get to work on fixing it.

Many people think that hoarseness is the only major sign of vocal injury. This is not the case. Breathiness, lack of resonance, reduced vocal endurance, and a sensation of increased effort can also suggest the possibility of mucosal injury. When an actor says that his voice is "tired", what he really should be saying is "my vocal fold mucosa is swollen" or "my voice is acutely injured." Use of incorrect terminology (like "my voice is tired") can lead certain performers "down the garden path" because they don't think about their voice problems correctly. Therefore, they don't do the right things to solve the problem or to prevent the vocal problem from reoccurring in the future.

When performers do not think accurately about the cause of their vocal problems (that is, illness versus injury) then problems arise in regard to how they are going to go about remedying their vocal distress. Patients who convince themselves that all their vocal problems are the result of colds or allergies, for example, will put their focus on finding an allergy pill or cold remedy rather than putting their attention on their vocal behavior and will not succeed in vocal rehabilitation.[1]

Otolaryngologist Dr. Friedrich Brodnitz, a renowned authority on voice disorders and author of *Keep Your Voice Healthy*, suggests that the professional actor/singer should "pick his throat specialist in healthy days and ask for a thorough checkup of all vocal organs. The doctor who has studied the patient's body under normal conditions and has observed, on various occasions, its reactions to infection, drugs, and treatments, is in a much better position to help than the once-consulted physician."[2] Indeed, an actor needs to give the selection of an otolaryngologist the same care and consideration that he gives to the selection of other members of his "support team"—his acting, voice, and movement teachers, as well as his agent and photographer. As

Dr. Bastian has pointed out, acting for the stage involves "high risk" vocal behavior. Having access to the expertise of an otolaryngologist who is familiar with the actor's vocal mechanism in sickness and in health and who understands the demands of the acting profession is of utmost importance in the maintenance of good vocal health and the actor's peace of mind.

Stress and the Actor

It is common knowledge that the actor's life is a stressful one. High unemployment and employment that is often inconsistent and unpredictable are the norm. Actors must learn to cope with the stress and psychological burdens that accompany professional insecurity and instability.

To a great extent, the actor's professional life is always at the dictates of someone else—a producer, director, or agent—and, for the actor, this entails a very real sense of lack of control over one's destiny. Even when employed in a production, the actor is not in a position of control—the director is. Only the director can oversee the whole of production. All the hard work of a good actor can be undermined by any one of the many theatrical elements, such as sound, lights, costumes, scenery, stage properties, other actors, or an auditorium that is too hot or too cold. Most actors know this and often expend a great deal of energy worrying about elements of production over which they have little or no control.

Actors often live with ongoing conflict between their personal and professional lives. "The show must go on" is not only a statement of theatrical spirit, it is a fact of life. If an actor does not appear for a performance due to some personal reason, he is either fired or, if the absence is justified, replaced temporarily by another actor. For the absent actor there is always the stressful possibility that the understudy will turn in a superior performance and thereby become a threat.

The skilled actor eliminates personal tension in performance by concentrating on the given circumstances of the role, but prior to total immersion in the character, many actors experience high levels of tension and anxiety concerning their upcoming performance. In this unstable profession, each performance can become for the actor, not merely a performance, but an audition for future employment. This is why actors are always asking the stage manager, "Who is in the house tonight? Did you see this critic, agent, director, or producer?" In his article "The Professional Voice" Dr. Robert Thayer Sataloff discusses the effects of stage fright upon the singer's voice, but his observations pertain to the actor as well.

The human voice is an exquisitely sensitive messenger of emotion. Highly trained singers learn to control the effects of anxiety and other emotional stresses on their voices under ordinary circumstances. However, in some instances this training may break down, or a performer may be inadequately prepared to control the voice under specific stressful conditions. Pre-performance anxiety, or stage fright, is the most common example; but insecurity, depression, and other emotional disturbances are also generally reflected in the voice. Anxiety reactions are mediated in part through the automatic nervous system and result in dry mouth, cold clammy skin and thick secretions. These reactions are normal, and good vocal training coupled with assurance that there is no abnormality or disease generally overcomes them. However, long-term, poorly compensated emotional stress and exogenous stress (from agents, producers, teachers, parents, etc.) may cause substantial vocal dysfunction and may result in permanent limitations of the vocal apparatus. These conditions must be diagnosed and treated expertly.[3]

Despite the uncertainty of the actor's employment, the actor is required to stay ever ready to perform. The body must be toned, and the voice must be trained. The acting technique must be kept honed, if not on the stage, then in acting classes. The audition monologues must be polished. The wardrobe, pictures, and resumés need to be updated, and the "rounds" must be made. And, above all, not only good health, but *physical hardiness* must be cultivated. Key to this latter requirement is learning how to manage stress, for stress can result in the actor's inattention to his health and lead to patterns of behavior that are harmful to his vocal and physical well-being.

Alcohol

A famous actor once said, "Theatre is the drink after the performance." The actor's work day usually ends after 11:00 P.M. when most of the working world has gone to sleep. Theatre is a communal art form and, after the play, many actors feel the need to continue the camaraderie with their fellow artists. The "cast party" or the trip to the local bar often provide the most accessible outlets for stress reduction and social interaction. In recent years actors, like our society as a whole, have become more concerned with health and fitness. But the practice of having a drink after the show is, for many, an integral part of the actor's life style. After performing, actors may feel highly energized or physically, mentally, and emotionally drained depending upon the nature of the play. Alcohol is often viewed by actors as a way "to come down" from the excitement of performance or a way to make the transition from the world of the play back to reality. The former view is a very real one and needs to be addressed in terms of healthier options. The latter view is reflective of the fact that the actor has not yet mastered the necessary technique of removing the character from his psyche as he removes his makeup and costume after the show.

As Dr. Brodnitz points out, if the actor/singer limits his "consumption of alcohol to an occasional drink *following* a performance and avoid[s] exposure to cold weather afterward, no harm is done."[4] But, in many cases, having a drink after the show is the worst possible option for the actor if the drinking takes place in a noisy environment. Parties and bars are often noisy places with loud music, talking, and smoke-filled air. Having already taxed his voice in performance, the last thing the actor needs is to continue heightened vocal activity into the wee hours of the morning. Yet, after many drinks, the actor may feel himself capable of shouting above the environmental noise and will engage, therefore, in such vocally abusive behavior. Dr. Robert Thayer Sataloff writes, "A history of alcohol abuse would suggest the probability of poor vocal technique. Intoxication results in poor coordination and decreased awareness, which undermine vocal discipline designed to optimize and protect the voice."[5] Dr. Sataloff's statement embodies the rationale for why it is an important part of the actor's professional discipline to refrain from alcohol consumption prior to a rehearsal or performance. But actors have not always given the same logical consideration to patterns of alcohol abuse after a performance.

In addition to drinking alcohol, many actors eat late at night after a performance and then go directly to bed. This habit can lead to a condition known as acid reflux laryngopharyngitis in which "stomach acid travels up to the level of the throat and may even come into contact with parts of the larynx during sleep and cause symptoms such as chronic sore throat (especially severe in the morning), excessive morning phlegm, a chronic irritative cough, a sensation of needing to continually clear one's throat, or a particularly low or husky morning voice requiring a prolonged warm-up for the actor/ singer."[6] As more and more actors receive voice training and are educated about vocal care, healthier options—a walk with colleagues, physical relaxation exercises, or a warm, relaxing bath—may begin to supplant the longstanding ritual of "having a drink" or heavy meal after the show.

Smoking

Given the frequently stressful nature of the actor's profession, it is not surprising that many actors become addicted to cigarettes. In the face of anxiety, frustration, emotionally intense rehearsals, or the boredom of waiting around to rehearse a scene, the actor seeks ways to "nourish" himself. Food and cigarettes are often regarded as the most readily available means of such "nourishment." Excessive eating leads, of course, to undesired weight gain. So, for many actors, cigarettes become a means of "getting ready" to rehearse, taking a break from rehearsal, "getting up" for performance, or "coming down" from the performance. These rationales for smoking only serve to justify for the actor what is, in fact, an addiction to nicotine.

The harmful effects of tobacco smoke on the vocal mechanism are well-documented. Tobacco contains at least three dangerous chemicals: tar, nicotine, and carbon monoxide. Both the smoke and the heat of the cigarette cause direct irritation to the mucous membranes of the vocal tract including the vocal folds, the trachea, and the bronchi. The heat of the cigarette has a drying effect. The smoke is drawn in right between the vocal folds in order to get into the trachea. The same factors that cause cancer and bronchitis and all the inflammatory diseases in the lungs can cause inflammatory changes in the vocal folds. When smoke is passed through the vocal folds, it tends to vasodilate (that is, cause dilation of the blood vessels) the vocal folds. When the vascularity of the vocal folds is increased, they go from a white color to a more pinkish coloration, and the speaker's vulnerability to vocal injury is heightened. In addition, excessive smoking can contribute to the formation of laryngeal polyps. Long term smokers are at risk of developing what are called "smoker's" polyps; that is, polyps of the vocal folds. Such persons develop low, gravelly sounding voices, often referred to as "cigarette and bourbon" voices. In light of all the available information regarding the unhealthful effects of smoking, it behooves the actor who smokes to give serious consideration to conquering this addiction. And, if the actor is unable to quit on his own, he should not hesitate to seek professional assistance.[7]

Even the nonsmoker in the theatre may find it difficult to escape the adverse effects of secondhand smoke. Many directors (as well as assistant directors and stage managers) chain smoke as they work, unmindful of the fact that the smoke is being inhaled by the actors throughout the rehearsal period. In general, actors like to stay on good terms with their directors and, unless they are securely established in the profession, may be hesitant to mention their discomfort and anxiety in such a situation. What is needed in the theatre is a heightened awareness, by all concerned, regarding the actor's vocal demands and vocal health.

The Vocal Director and the Actor's Vocal Health

It is not the function of the vocal director to take responsibility for an actor's personal health habits; they are just that—the actor's *personal* responsibility. The vocal director can, however, help to educate actors regarding vocal care in the initial orientation session of the rehearsal process and share information with the actors regarding the maintenance of vocal health when asked. But to comment on an actor's personal behavior off the stage oversteps the bounds of professional decorum. The vocal director is responsible solely for what goes on vocally upon the stage.

As has been discussed, instances of vocal misuse, overuse, or abuse within the rehearsal process and in performance need to be carefully monitored by the vocal director to insure each actor's healthful functioning as a member of the production. In this professional capacity, the vocal director represents, along with the actors' own discipline and knowledge of vocal technique, a "first line of defense" against vocal abuse and acute vocal injury. If an actor suffers from a chronic vocal indisposition such as vocal fatigue, hoarseness, or breathiness and these problems cannot be remedied by alterations in the actor's vocal technique, then the vocal director, in consultation with the actor and the director, may choose to recommend that the actor be examined by an otolaryngologist. In such instances, is very helpful if the vocal director has already identified otolaryngologists in the area who have a background in working with performing artists, so that he can assist the actor in finding a physician, if the actor does not already have one.

Notes

1. From the author's December 5, 1989 interview with Dr. Robert Bastian, otolaryngologist and professor in the Department of Otolaryngology—Head and Neck Surgery—at the Loyola University of Chicago Medical Center, Maywood, Illinois.

2. Dr. Friedrich Brodnitz, *Keep Your Voice Healthy* (Boston: College Hill Press, 1988), p. 93.

3. Dr. Robert Thayer Sataloff, "The Professional Voice: Part I. Anatomy, Function, and General Health," *Journal of Voice*, Vol. 1, No. 1, (New York: Raven Press, 1987), pp. 98–99.

4. Brodnitz, *Keep Your Voice Healthy*, p. 74.

5. Sataloff, "The Professional Voice: Part I. Anatomy, Function, and General Health," p. 100.

6. Excerpted from "Laryngitis and Sore Throats From Acid Reflux," a description of the condition and suggestions for treatment provided by the Department of Otolaryngology, Loyola University Mulcahy Outpatient Center, Maywood, Illinois 60153.

7. From the author's interview with Dr. Robert Bastian on December 5, 1989.

Chapter 7

Final Thoughts

Because vocal direction is relatively new to the American theatre, vocal directors are frequently called upon to educate other theatre artists about their work as well as to do the work itself. Given this fact, there are some additional thoughts which need to be discussed in regard to the vocal director's work and how directors view the work of the theatre voice specialist in production.

For much too long in the American theatre, the art of acting has been taught in isolation from voice and movement training. This is what Harold Clurman was referring to when he expressed his concern that American teachers of the "Method" had "gotten stuck in the thirties [and] 'ghettoized' the American actor"[1] by focusing solely on the actor's psychology in the creation of a role. The reality, of course, is that the actor's instrument is made up of his mind and body. The voice is a critical part of the actor's physical instrument, and it is the responsibility of those who work with actors' voices in the theatre to bring to the work a knowledge of the science of vocal production as well as how the voice functions to serve the actor as an interpretive artist.

Until all students of acting and directing include in their education the study of voice production and care, abusive vocal practices will continue to occur in acting classes and play rehearsals. Lighting designers would not think of wiring theatrical lighting equipment without a knowledge of electricity. But many directors and teachers of acting manipulate actors' vocal instruments every day without any knowledge of how the human voice functions. A stage combat specialist is readily brought in to choreograph a sword fight, but a "screaming" match between two actors frequently occurs in rehearsals without the presence of a stage voice specialist. The theatre is an ephemeral art form; plays open and close and are gone forever. But the actor's vocal instrument goes on, either strengthened and developed by the experience, or abused and diminished in its capacity. The presence of a vocal director, highly educated in both the art and science of the speaking voice, helps to insure that the latter is not the unfortunate result of the actor's theatrical experience.

In the creation of a character for the stage, the way an actor moves, the sounds he makes, the words he speaks, and the way he utters them are a direct reflection of that actor's inner experience and understanding of the role. Often, however, when an actor focuses solely on capturing the inner truth of a role in performance, he does not effectively utter the character's words; he mutters them, with no recognition of the fact that language in the theatre must be actively shared with the audience. One of the challenges of the stage actor is to utilize his voice in such a way as to have a visceral and emotional effect upon the audience; either through the way the actor, as character, addresses another character or by the way the actor addresses the audience. The ability to vocally share a character's inner thoughts and feelings with an audience requires great skill on the part of the actor and expert guidance on the part of the director and vocal director. The more stage directors, as well as vocal directors, learn about how to listen and how human thought and feeling are communicated through the sound of the actor's voice, the more they will be able to help guide actors in using their voices in ways that audiences find aestheticaly pleasing, exciting, moving, and enlightening.

At some point in the rehearsal process, the stage director needs to become aware of how the play's language is being delivered; how the actors are making use of stress, inflection, word coloration, and tone to communicate to the audience the characters' inner lives. This aspect of the actor's performance is, of course, a major concern of the vocal director. Some directors do not understand the work of the vocal director and often assume that vocal directors engage in making interpretive decisions regarding line delivery. These directors may feel that, when a vocal director assists an actor in bringing clarity to a line, they are intruding on the director's domain. On the contrary, the vocal director must continually listen to the actor to determine if the actor knows what his lines mean. A major function of the stage director is to decide what the play is about and to make a decision regarding the way the play is going to be realized in production. Once the director's vision for production is made clear to all members of the production team, it is their responsibility to analyze the language of the text to determine how the director's concept for production is to be realized. The set designer examines the text to understand the physical world of the play. The lighting designer studies the play to discern patterns of actor movement as well as atmospheric and environmental shifts. And the vocal director analyzes the text to determine how the play's language is to be spoken in light of the director's vision for production. In rehearsal, the vocal director continually listens to the actors to discern 1) if the actors are interpreting their lines in accordance with the director's interpretation and 2) if the lines and their intrinsic meaning are being communicated with clarity for an audience. When a vocal director gives an actor a note that enhances the clarity of his line delivery, it is by no means an infringement upon the director's domain as interpreter and acting coach. It is, quite simply, the vocal director's job. Again, this is why close collaboration between the vocal and stage directors and the concept of "thinking as one" are so critical, for it is not only the play's text, but also the director's vision for production that gives focus to the work of the vocal director.

One very disturbing trend in today's theatre requires the attention of directors, actors, designers, and vocal directors alike. This is the encroaching and frequently arbitrary electronic amplification of actors' voices. Common sense dictates that, when theatres are poorly designed in terms of acoustics, when the size of a theatre auditorium prevents the actors from projecting without strain, when a live band or orchestra accompanies the actors' singing, or when the production has been musically scored with electronic amplification in mind, sound reinforcement is necessary to insure the vocal health of the actor. But, when stage actors are miked for nonmusical productions because they have insufficient vocal skills or because the notion that today's audiences, so accustomed to the recorded sound of film and television, will readily accept, and even prefer, the presence of electronic amplification, dangerous precedents are being set. In providing indiscriminate sound reinforcement for actors in the theatre, we are denying what is "live" about "live" theatre and are stripping away one of the theatre's most powerful attributes and appeals—the natural sound of the human voice.

Many years ago, my mother told me how, as a young child, she had attended a touring company's production of *Macbeth* and was deeply affected by the actor playing Malcolm who, upon hearing of the slaughter of his wife and children, had uttered the words "All my pretty ones? Did you say all? O hell-kite! All?"[2] My mother would imitate the actor's moaning, incredulous utterance of the word "all," and each time she told the story, her eyes would fill with tears, and she would seem to be reliving the experience of decades past. Indeed, every theatre-goer can recount moments when an actor's voice or the way an actor delivered a line evoked an unforgettable moment of insight, joy, laughter, or pain; a moment when the sound of an actor's voice communicated directly to the hearts and minds of the audience some truth regarding the human experience.

Speaking to the actor in his book *The Dramatic Imagination,* Robert Edmond Jones states that:

> Great roles require great natures to interpret them. Half our pleasure in
> seeing a play lies in our knowledge that we are in the presence of artists.
> But this pleasure of watching the artists themselves is soon forgotten, if
> the play is well performed, in the contagious excitement of watching a

miracle: the miracle of incarnation. . . . Just as the good designer retires in favor of the actor, so does the good actor withdraw his personal self in favor of the character he is playing. He steps aside. The character lives in him. You are to play Hamlet. Then you become his host. You invite him into yourself. You lend him your body, your voice, your nerves; but it is Hamlet's voice that speaks, Hamlet's impulses that move you. . . . To spend a lifetime in practicing and perfecting the art of speaking in tongues other than one's own is to live as greatly as one can live.[3]

As students of acting soon come to realize, becoming a great actor demands much more than an innate talent and desire. To create the life of another human being for the stage, as seen by the playwright, requires not only "great natures," but consumate artistry and technical skill. As Laurence Olivier once said, "If you are an artist, you must *prove* it,"[4] and it is the challenge of the stage actor to "prove it" with a high degree of success and consistency performance after performance. If actors are equipped to meet this challenge—psychologically, vocally, and physically—then their lives in the theatre will include "miracles of incarnation" and will surpass a limited and ultimately boring expression of their own personalities.

To assist actors in "practicing and perfecting the art of speaking in tongues other than [their] own" is, for the vocal director, a richly rewarding experience. Studying and listening to the language of our dramatic poets, participating in the collaborative process of bringing clarity and meaningful life to a play in production, and hearing the wonderous and limitless ways in which an actor's voice can express and illuminate human nature all contribute to the joy of practicing the art of vocal direction for the theatre.

Notes

1. Charles Marowitz, *Prospero's Staff* (Bloomington and Indianapolis: Indiana University Press, 1986), p. 79.

2. William Shakespeare, *Macbeth,* ed. by Sylvan Barnet (New York: The New American Library, Inc., 1963), p. 113.

3. Robert Edmond Jones, *The Dramatic Imagination* (New York: Theatre Arts Books, 1941), pp. 31–33.

4. From Melvyn Bragg's interview with Sir Laurence Olivier contained in the television special "Laurence Olivier—A Life—," a South Bank Show Special and part of the Great Performances series, produced and directed by Bob Bee.

Index